The Elements of Song Craft

The Contemporary Songwriter's Usage Guide to Writing Songs That Last

BILLY SEIDMAN

Guilford, Connecticut

Published by Backbeat Books
An imprint of The Rowman & Littlefield Publishing Group, Inc.
4501 Forbes Blvd., Ste. 200
Lanham, MD 20706
www.rowman.com

Distributed by NATIONAL BOOK NETWORK

GPS, Audience Tracking, Song Intention, and Core Emotion icons made by Freepik from www.flaticon.com. Song Category icon made by Pixel Perfect from www.flaticon.com.

Library of Congress Cataloging-in-Publication Data available

ISBN 978-1-4930-4765-9 (paperback)
ISBN 978-1-4930-5078-9 (e-book)

In memory of Richard "Rick" Depofi 1957–2018.

His honesty was a songwriter's best friend.

Contents

It's the lyrics that makes a song a hit,
although the tune, of course, is what makes it last.

—Irving Berlin

Preface

The phone rang one afternoon in Nashville. The voice on the other end introduced himself, "Billy, this is Bobby Braddock, I'm calling to let you know I like this song of yours, "A Circle Has No Sides," very much, it's a real fine song. I'm not sure there's a place for it on Blake's record, but it caught my attention and I wanted to thank you for sending it over." Bobby Braddock is a giant among Nashville songwriters; he had discovered a new artist, Blake Shelton, and was preparing to produce his first album. I'd seen Blake a few times. He was easy to notice: slim, willowy, tall, a big "green to the business, happy to be here" grin on his face. He was partial to wearing a black duster and wide-brimmed hat, walking from the big house (Sony's main office) 'cross the parking lot to the "firehouse," a former fire station turned into Sony/ATV Music Publishing, Nashville's writer rooms.

It was a bittersweet call, hearing from a legend who had liked but passed on a song. A week earlier, I had pitched "A Circle Has No Sides" to a storied, producer-publisher who literally leapt from his chair proclaiming, "That's a hit song if ever I heard one!" This is what encouragement looks like at a midlevel position in a songwriter's career: signed to a publisher, poised for but not yet breaking through with a major cut.

It turns out "A Circle Has No Sides" wasn't finished; there was one line missing, a line I rewrote ten or so years later that came to me on a mountaintop in Tibet, of all places. The new line I wrote was: "I wish I was more like the wind, I'd soar where eagles fly." The line it replaced was: "I wish I was more like the truth, I wouldn't tell so many lies."

I hadn't written enough songs in Nashville yet to see this glaring mistake when I wrote "A Circle Has No Sides." First, no artists want to say or admit they tell too many lies; and second, that's not a line inviting listeners into a song or one listeners want to or can see "their life" in. (Especially in a song reminding people of the best qualities they have in common.)

I learned from this mistake and many others, thanks to the years lived in Nashville and the great writers I wrote/write with who hipped me to "write up!"

"Writing up" to one's full potential is what *The Elements of Song Craft* is designed to do.

If you're a new or developing songwriter, one who've written between ten and ninety songs, the book is designed for you. It offers strategies, tactics, and methods to write songs from the bottom up; that is, to harness the power of universal emotions quickly and effectively, so the songs can produce a state of Emotional Hypnotism™ in a listener.

That's the effect good or great songs have: they hypnotize us! There is no thinking involved. There's reaction, pure emotional reaction.

If you're an experienced songwriter, there's also much to gain, apply, or confirm about the art of songwriting from the flow of information and perspectives offered throughout the book, which can be put to work in your songs.

Quality songs have been built for eons by the great songwriters of the past and the top songwriters of today. The methods and strategies here represent experienced choices the heroes of song made and make in navigating passion and craft, head and heart, to connect deeply with an audience.

Applying standards of excellence matters if your goal is to connect with large audiences.

Analyze a good or great songwriter and you'll find avid students of song. They have songwriting heroes, they've studied their songs, they've learned the rules, they've broken the rules, all leading to the creation of a signature personal style, an alchemy of musical and lyrical vocabulary unique to them.

You're in one business if you're a songwriter: the communications business.

How prized communication is to a songwriter shows up over time. How? By writing lots of songs and then seeing their effect; they hypnotize the audience! Communication is the standard for a good song. Good beginnings matter in songwriting because the form is so short and direct; there's no time to get anything wrong. So, let's discuss our good beginning . . .

What makes a song last? What is the DNA, the essential strands that bind together emotion, words, melody, music, and sound so they last and matter to audiences over time?

Answering that in depth would take a book in itself, but simply put, I believe songs last for a few key reasons.

Why Songs Last

1. They're lyrically and musically exceedingly well conceived and written, meaning they contain both elements of surprise and familiarity, honesty, originality, images, and statements, or a twist/variation on a previously conceived famous song, which are then directed toward the right audience (an audience that either needs to hear or finds comfort in the song's message and feel).

2. They time-stamp either a generational or an individual experience; for example, songs by the Beatles that served for an entire generation, or "that" summer song you partied or fell in love to.

3. They contain a timeless melody that captures our emotions magically, all by itself, a melody that seemingly tells a story; for example, "Greensleeves," "Yesterday," the "Moonlight" Sonata.

4. They capture the mood or essence of times (past or present) when the emotional stakes (loss or hope) are extraordinarily high for people. Examples: catastrophic events, such as WWI, the 1918 pandemic, the market crash of 1929, WWII, and crushingly the 2020 pandemic (happening as this book goes to print)—changing and reshaping what life looks and feels like for millions of people.

5. They capture a time of seemingly deep peacefulness and emotion ease and stability; for example, the classic 1963 bossa nova recordings of Getz and Gilberto.

6. They seamlessly take advantage of our inborn need and connection to storytelling and our natural recognition of literary and musical structures and forms.

These seem to be a few of the conditions in which many songs with longevity are born, where great writers have stepped up and represent the deepest human emotions and/or needs simply, directly, and without pretense.

Every decision in songwriting matters: balancing instinct with craft, experience with happenstance, pictures with statements, storytelling with documentation.

That said, there are two major issues facing developing songwriters.

Issues Developing Songwriters Face

- Confusing how good it feels to write a song with how good the song actually is

- Aiming too low with a song's reason for being; that is, not being initially ambitious enough in choosing a song's concept or reason to exist

For example, David Bowie aimed so high in his writing ambitions, he became one of the pioneers/inventors of glam rock. So, how high are you aiming? It's a good question, because one needs a combination of talent, experience, vision/ambition, a strong work ethic, and luck to have a shot at writing a song that could last.

—

Two factors led to the writing of this book. The first was reading *The Elements of Style,* which my mom, an English teacher and poet, introduced me to when I was a teenager. The second was my move to Nashville, Tennessee, in the midnineties.

I like to call Nashville the "Hollywood of songwriting craft" for the simple reason that it has been a magnet attracting some of the finest singer-songwriters and songwriter-craftsman for generations. (Side note: Texas is the ancient Greece of American songwriting!)

Breathing the air, drinking the water there, driving around town day in and day out, listening to the radio, I discovered something quite startling. Even though I'd been writing songs for many years prior, I'd never understood something so elemental about how you could put a song together with such devastating emotional power.

I'd get eight or fifteen seconds into listening to a song and *bam*, my life was at stake, my future was in the balance, my joy or heartbreak was pouring out of me. And all it took was several seconds! How did these new songwriting heroes of mine write songs that did that?! It became my quest and my passion to find out.

The answer was this: great songs are written from a much deeper emotional place from the very beginning. The good writers really know what they're writing about and why, long before they start connecting all the wires, crafting, and putting their songs together.

Of course, there are happy musical and lyrical accidents, gifts from the muse, as well as challenging musical and lyrical curves to navigate. But ultimately, what's complex about this process is that you've got to write a lot of songs; you've got to exercise this perception, this knowledge to develop it and keep your instincts sharp.

Songs are imbedded into culture the way fossils are into rock formations. Each generation inherits from the previous the intuitive nature of knowing storytelling and song form. Songs are then rebuilt with slight variations of titles, lyrics, melody, rhythm, and form. The songs that have come before set the rules and also set a baseline for creative rule breakers.

This book is subversive in that it is a guide to writing good songs, but something deeper and unexpected can happen by practicing the strategies, formulas, prompts, and exercises in it.

There's the opportunity to learn how to be exceptionally present in the moment, to witness and report back to your audience (in song) the Emotional Transactions™ happening around them every day that everyone seemed to miss but you!

Once this sensitivity is acquired, a writer can write songs in a way that matters most to listeners. Why? Because, much like how an acoustic instrument develops a richer sound from years of being played, years of training yourself to be present exercises your writer's heart.

It becomes a practiced habit to discover which of your emotions register deepest and need the most thorough expression; these are the emotions that will affect your audience's emotions.

Learning to stay present in the moment to witness the Emotional Transactions happening around me was one of the great songwriting gifts I received from Nashville.

This is where good writers live, making valuations of the human experience and their own, the connecting of heart and head, employing a unique writing style and a vocabulary with images at once familiar and unexpected, and oh, by the way . . . possessing the craft to pull the miracle off!

Introduction

Standards matter. This book is designed to keep high standards always in front of you while navigating the wilderness and range of your lyrical and musical passions and ideas regardless of genre.

Ideas do the heavy lifting in songwriting. A good idea does 50 percent of the lift; a great idea, 75 percent; and an extraordinary idea, 90 percent. You still need the craft skills—the ability to execute the idea—to get in the trench and connect all the wires lyrically and musically to finish the job. But ultimately, it is the idea that matters most.

Good beginnings are essential in songwriting. So, how do we distinguish among a good, great, and extraordinary idea?

A large part of making that distinction is this: all good writers should know the shape of their heart, meaning they should know what themes empower and ring true to them. Typically, such themes as justice, hope, regret, joy, loss, grief, longing, reassurance, empowerment, gratitude, alienation, anger, relief, revenge, partying, confidence, or swagger form the basis of many songs. These are life's big themes and emotions.

Know what acts or emotions reassure or frighten you and which comfort or repulse you, and you'll have a unique place from which to begin reaching an audience. Why? Because knowing the shape of your own heart is how you'll reach into the hearts of others.

Practical realities: it takes writing a lot of songs to get good at executing ideas. This is the part that's often left out, overlooked, or omitted when developing writers get excited about their developing song—the plan.

Within a large population, there are those few who possess the balance to write a great or brilliant song fresh out of the box—a song that would take most writers years to perfect. In my experience, that's exceedingly rare. It's the Songwriting Athletes™, those who work tirelessly at the art and craft by writing dozens upon dozens of songs, who grow their perception and skill at songwriting. It is these songwriters who arrive at a place where their songs consistently stand up and people notice their talent.

To that end, *The Elements of Song Craft* is a songwriting athletes' manual of the core processes of songwriting.

What follows is a thorough reveal of the tools, perspectives, distinctions, and strategies used by countless generations of songwriters for an emerging generation of serious writers to build their musical and lyrical craft skills with.

Many chapters include prompts for writing original songs, using the craft tools presented in those chapter. Although optional, the prompts provide an opportunity to greatly improve one's songwriting skill and practice.

Each chapter introduces new craft tools and prompts designed and road-tested to help writers accelerate their songwriting perception and athleticism.

The chapters build on one another until a dynamic system emerges that ties the essential elements and practices used in creating memorable songs.

The charts, graphs, musical examples, lists, and "one-sheets" throughout are visual aids showing the relationship between creating ideas and options for how best to write them for maximum impact on audiences.

As the book contains numerous lyrical and musical examples of songs to critique and study, an audio companion *Elements of Song Craft* YouTube Channel and Spotify playlist have been created for readers to listen to and review as part of their song analysis. The ▶ icon next to a song's title indicates its inclusion on the playlists.

Elements YouTube Channel playlist:

https://music.youtube.com/playlist?list=PLfZkFVqzU4Q5AJNCtphLeJjgYH014wQb8

Elements Spotify Playlist: https://open.spotify.com/playlist/01GSrO1VT94AyPO3pdYl3f

The *Elements* also contains a condensed reference section highlighting the core strategies found in the book. This section (part two) is designed for songwriters on the go to quickly reference practical and concise songwriting decision making related to:

- Song concept development

- Title ideation and lyric creation

- Lyrical editorial tools

- Melody (topline) creation

- Lyrical and musical momentum strategies

- Musical composition strategies

- Lyrical and musical rewriting strategies

Part two can be used before, during, or after writing sessions for inspiration, making smart craft choices, or for creative problem-solving solutions.

Taken together, parts one and two create a context for reinventing how to listen to songs, to identify their strengths or weaknesses, and then ably apply this knowledge to your own songwriting.

Learning to leave out everything that doesn't matter and leave in everything that does, draws an audience close, keeps them listening, then keeps a song in their heart and memories long after it's finished playing. Isn't that the goal of a good songwriter, creating a little immortality? Let's get to work at aiming that high!

—Billy Seidman
New York City 2020

Part One

The
Elements
of
Song Craft

1

Lyric Development

You're a Songwriter, So What Business Are You In?

Hands down, the best communicators throughout history have always been songwriters.

Long before books or printing presses, songwriters plied their trade practicing and refining communication as art. In fact, what other writer historically can claim to stir such intense feelings of joy, loss, hope, forgiveness, regret, or reassurance in ten seconds or less?

I call this ability **Emotional Hypnotism**. Under the snake charm of a good songwriter, the audience never sees this art at work, but the emotions the charm casts remains alive in their head and heart long after the music fades—the proof being the power of a melody's ability to bring to life a long-forgotten memory. This is what a unique communication achievement does.

The art of emotional hypnosis has been practiced by musicians, songwriters, and shamans for millennia and beyond. The troubadours of the twelfth and thirteenth centuries were early practitioners. (Some, as history records, the sons of titled nobility, were "bitten" by the songwriting bug just as songwriters are today.)

Either you have an audience for your songs or you don't. Our songwriter brethren quickly figured how to best capture and keep an audience's attention by reflecting in song and verse, their joys, delights, and fears. They developed songwriting techniques to captivate their audiences. They spread the news, were topical, funny, bawdy, tender, and entertaining. In a phrase, they knew what people needed and wanted to hear.

Who were mankind's first newscasters, gossip columnists, political satirists, and populist communications experts? Songwriters!

Cut to hundreds of years later, when books, YouTube; how-to videos; online learning, and presentations on business, creative writing, marketing, or branding spell out that anyone looking to be persuasive needs to understand how to communicate effectively.

But we songwriters are in many respects the founding fathers of popular communication art. Our tools are prodigious, even subversive in the hands of the best of us, so developing writers take note: What business are you in? The communications business!

Communication is the gold standard for songwriters. There's no explaining to an audience what you meant. Developing songwriters may feel dispirited or discouraged when the response to a new song played for a friend or family member is, "I don't like it," "I don't get it," "Umm, that's cute; what else you got?" especially when what you wrote seemed so clear to you.

This is a rite of passage for all songwriters. I say, brush off that momentary disappointment and start to embrace two practical realities of songwriting:

- The proof you successfully communicated in your song lies in the listener's understanding and takeaway.

- You honestly searched your heart for subjects you needed and wanted to write about, and found an audience that needed and wanted to hear it.

Without having the experience of writing a lot of songs, developing songwriters face two unique challenges to communicating effectively:

- It feels so good to write a song, we confuse how good it feels to write the song with how good the song actually is.

- Developing songwriters often times aim too low in their song's ambition, meaning a song's title or theme is not sufficiently unique, timely, bold, clear, thought through, exciting, interesting, poetic, honest, or relevant enough to garner avid audience attention for the song from its very inception.

Even with our ability to use music as a component to hypnotize, if our song's theme selection is unclear or underwhelming, the song faces the likelihood of an early crib death due to its failure to find an audience to claim it for its own.

You're the first audience member. You determine what's good, relevant, or worthy, but guess what?

Our judgment is often off the table in this initial writing period I call **The Creation Space™**.

So, what's the hedge? How can you best manage or intercede on these challenges to good songwriting? The hedge is *song craft*: writing a lot of songs using the craft and smart decision-making processes songwriters have historically employed to win mass audiences for their music.

For example, a primary craft tool historically used to write better lyrics is knowing where in your lyrics you can summarize what you've written, so as to spell out for the audience why you've said what you've said.

Summarizing, or **Summing Up™**, is tied to song form and is easy to see in action once you're taught to recognize it.

Summing Up clears up any confusion an audience might have about your intent.

It's a form of **Lyrical Grammar™**, just one of many critiquing tools in this book.

Another critical craft tool is the use of musical and lyrical momentum. Just as figure skaters score higher marks for the speed in which they deliver their routines, so to do songwriters.

Creating great momentum, calculating the **Distance To Target™** (the time it takes to introduce your song's theme early in a first verse, and then its title in the chorus) is probably the thought that consumes most accomplished songwriters as they sort out and determine the road map of their song (once convinced they're got a song/idea/title worth writing).

All writers have a process or develop one. Start with a title, a few words, wing a riff or musical motif; sing a melody, sing random improvised words or made up sounds to a melody, write a melody to an overheard phrase, get inspired by a beat, a chord progression, a slamming track—it all works when looking to get a basic toehold on the mountain of the idea or emotion you're exploring. That's the natural process, but it's also where many writers stop planning for a fruitful outcome for the rest of their song.

Experienced songwriters have many advantages at this point in a song's development. They have the experience to stay in their "songwriting process" and get the job done right. The signposts pointing to their song's opportunity and final destination are well known to them because they've written so many, but also they have the ability to listen deeply to the developing song itself. They're able to figure out what kind of song they are writing, what else needs to be said, and what doesn't need to be said to make it well written.

With so much to know, what decisions are critical to achieving feats of communication alchemy early in the writing process?

- Write your songs so people can see their life in them.

- Use images/pictures, metaphors, simile, analogy, and allegory liberally; they're sticky, whereas statements are less sticky.

With practice and dedication to learning song craft, you learn the art of performing Emotional Hypnotism on your audience. This book is designed to teach you the strategies, formulas, and craft needed to practice Emotional Hypnotism on people listening to your songs by:

- Teaching you new ways of listening to songs by "growing your ears," to recognize the great craft decisions good songwriters make.

- Being fully committing to staying emotionally honest in your writing and using your vulnerability as a core strength. Build a world-class BS detector.

- Using and gaining mastery of the dozen or so song craft tools that will ground you in good practices.

- Writing 6 to 20 songs using the principles, exercises, and writing prompts in this book. They've been specifically designed and road-tested for that purpose. They work, and will make you a better writer.

- Learning to love the discipline of rewriting your songs.

- Making a commitment to becoming a songwriting athlete.

I call this **Songwriting Athleticism**.

Olympic athletes train six hours a day. Pre-med, pre-law, nursing, and other professionals train extensively for many years to learn and excel at their professions, but somehow because music is often more associated with feeling, and because it just feels so good, sometimes songwriters get the idea that's enough, that skill and training aren't necessary as long as the feeling is there.

In songwriting, we build perception; that's our muscle. Much as how sound waves bouncing off the interior of a violin, cello, or guitar over many years makes the instrument sound richer tonally, so too do songwriters with years of writing under their belt develop a head-heart intelligence for smart, craft-heart decision making and a killer instinct for strong lyrical and musical ideas.

There's huge potential and opportunity in ideas and emotions, including the opportunity to harvest all of a song's DNA, the many strands of emotion and craft forming the essence of a song's idea.

Songwriting Athleticism builds and strengthens the needed craft and perception skills used to write good songs and leads to aiming extremely high in your writing ambitions.

The simple truth is that people are searching for themselves in your songs; you just need to know how to hold the mirror at eye level so they can see themselves.

To borrow a phrase from an old friend, Joe Cerisano, "Words are the one thing you can't buy at the guitar center," so if you want to write songs that matter to people, you'd better have a tried-and-true strategy to write lyrics that can win an audience for your music.

⦿ Intention

The best songwriters in the world think about songs very differently than do most people. They're masters of an emotional and intellectual three-dimensional chess game played between the head and the heart. They're well practiced at sizing up the many opportunities living in their ideas and then figuring out how "big" they can write that idea/emotion. As songwriting athletes, they've written hundreds of songs, been students of song, studied their heroes, collaborated, sifted through ideas, developed ideas, stumbled across ideas of value. They have a long history of using the craft skills described in this book, albeit perhaps with different names or vocabulary.

The result is an ability to shape ideas and feelings into songs that pay off with maximum effect on listeners.

Like the painter-sculptor Michelangelo, who famously said he could see the finished statue in the right piece of marble, good songwriters quickly select their right marble—the right idea, the right emotion, the right song category, then carve it into a finished work of art; a memorable song based on interest, need, inspiration, and craft.

If your goal is to become a great songwriter, you'll need to clearly see and understand the opportunities living in the marble of your ideas and your emotions. You'll need to understand your intention.

What do you want to have happen by writing or singing the song? What response, emotion, or feeling do you want the audience to have when they hear it? What's at stake for you writing or singing it? What deeper intention or emotion might be lying beneath a casual encounter with the song? What's essential to say about the idea? Why is it so important, urgent, or interesting for you to write it? What emotion is really at its core, driving it? Why will people care and want to hear it?

This brings us to a "Come to Jesus moment" as songwriters. What's in your heart? What themes or emotions do you wrestle with or explore? What feelings and thoughts keep you up at night, bring you joy, make you laugh? What inspires you to write in your journal or notes?

Good writers have learned to first look into their own heart to understand how best to communicate with and look into the hearts of others. I call this *knowing the shape of your heart,* as in knowing the themes, subjects, emotions, issues, and stories that ring so true in a writer's heart that causes them to have to write.

Knowing the shape of your heart will reveal, in significant ways, the patterns of "how" your intention, urgency, interest, and emotions show up in your songs. That's why so many writers use an intention-based songwriting approach, as intention helps to determine a long laundry list of opportunities present in your ideas. (An approach which is quite different from a **Free Association Song**™ writing style that we'll review in a later chapter.)

That being said, an idea or an intention by itself is not enough; *your song needs a finish line, a destination,* as well as being clearly written.

Audiences should not have to excessively hunt and peck, searching for a song's meaning. Hunting and pecking causes thinking; thinking *kills a song's momentum*; whereas feeling greases a song's wheels and advances Emotional Hypnotism.

Writing three or four random lyric lines that in your head hold meaning and are perfectly clear to you, does not guarantee they are clear to an audience, so don't assume the audience always "gets it."

Trains don't go wildly roaming the countryside; they're on tracks and have destinations. Your audience needs to know your song's destination, and fast. They need to know in five to fifteen seconds whether they're getting on that train and riding it with you. Song form is so short, you've got to lay down that track and make the destination clear.

Helping to align your intention is the craft tool Creative GPS™. Much like how standard GPS uses three vectors—where you are, where you're going/your destination, and how fast you're traveling toward it, Creative GPS uses vectors to "track" your song's development while under construction. Three of the vectors are based on decisions made prior to writing the song:

- **Song Intention:** Why are you writing it and what you want to have happen by writing/singing it?

- **Core Emotion:** What emotion is at the song's heart, driving it? What emotion do you want an audience to feel when they listen?

- **Song Category:** What type of song are you writing? For example, is the song a new love, devotional love, empowerment, coming of age song, etc.

And a fourth vector tracks how deeply your audience is staying in tune with the message or intention of the song throughout its length, through your use of song craft:

- **Audience Tracking™:** A list of continuous craft decisions that make sure listeners are continuously involved in the song and not getting off the train before the song reaches its destination.

The Elements of Song Craft Creative GPS™

1. **Intention:** What do you want to have happen by writing/singing the song? You're writing the song because you want . . . what?

2. **Core Emotion:** What core emotion is your song built on? What emotion are you feeling that you want your audience to feel?

3. **Song Category:** What song category does the song easily fit into?

Now that you know what kind of song you're writing, let's look at:

4. **Audience Tracking:** Which song craft tools will you use to invite your audience into the song and keep them emotionally hypnotized throughout the **song form**? From **Verse 1**, **Pre-chorus**, **Chorus**, **Verse 2**, **Bridge**, or **Refrain**, how are you balancing creativity and clarity in crafting the songs appeal to your audience?

Underlying Song Craft Distinctions

1. Songs are written as a response to an event.

2. Early in the writing process, make a conscious decision to put yourself on the "listener's" side of your song.

3. Standards matter! You're in the communication business. How well are you communicating your intention?

Applying Creative GPS as a Song Analysis Tool

Ed Sheeran and Amy Hodges's "Thinking Out Loud" serves as a solid contemporary song to demonstrate how Creative GPS works. Let's determine its:

♟ Song Intention

Hey, Ed! What do you want to happen by singing "Thinking Out Loud"?

Ed might respond, *"I want to persuade a woman of the deep love I have and the fidelity I will show her throughout our life together."*

♟♟ Core Emotion

What's the core emotion living at the heart of the song driving it?

Commitment

♫ Song Category

What song category does the song easily fall into?

It's a devotional love song.

👥 Audience Tracking

What craft tools are used in the song to get the audience to relate deeply to the song (i.e., see their life in it throughout the songs development)?

1. By singing in the second person, singing right to the girl herself, addressing her as "you." (When an audience hears "you," it works as if being addressed directly and brings them into the song.)

2. By the use of "Summing Up" in the song's first prechorus.

3. The use of singing *action command pictures* in the chorus, which adds momentum, contrast, and urgency to the song's development and chorus payoff

4. By, in the second verse, flipping the script to say how as he ages, he'll remain loving her. This keeps harvesting the intent of the first verse and keeps the song focused and simple; no need to add a new idea.

Using Creative GPS keeps a developing songs solidly on the rails. It ensures you're off to the right start by giving a song parameters that define the kind of song it is and the audience it's aimed at.

Harnessing the Power of the Song Arts Academy (SAA) Critiquing System

There's an effective way to identify the right marble, the right intention, or idea from which to begin carving your songs. This **Critiquing System**™, created for Song Arts Academy, helps writers develop the sensitivity to consistently see the core emotion at the heart of songs, the emotion causing an audience to react and feel.

Here's how it works. Each time you listen to a song, ask yourself these questions, then write down and study your answers:

A	B
	Song Mechanics
	Make a laundry list of every detail you notice about the musical and lyrical construction of the song you're critiquing, including:
1. If you could boil what you think this song is about into one word, **one emotion**, what emotion is it?	1. Which notes are sung or held long? (legato)
2. What does the person singing the song want to have happen by singing the song? They're singing the song because they want . . . **what?**	2. Which notes are sung short? (staccato)
	3. Which notes are sung loud or soft?
	4. What's the song's rhyme scheme?
	5. How is repetition showing up in the song?
	6. What do lyric lines have in common or where is there variation or repetition?
	7. Where in the song does the writer "sum up" before adding a new lyrical idea?
	8. What is the song's "song form?"
	9. How is the concept of the song, its emotional essence being shown in pictures?
	10. How is musical and lyrical momentum building throughout each section of the song's verses, prechorus, chorus, bridge, or refrain?
A song may be about love or pain, but love and pain are not descriptive enough for our purposes. Strive to "Drill Down" to discover what Core Emotion™ the song is resting on, typically; Hope, Joy, Loss, Grief, Regret, Rejection, & Reassurance among other core emotions.	Use the Song Mechanic questions to uncover clues to which core emotion lies at the heart of each song you listen to going forward . . .

Well-written songs are powered by very straightforward emotions, such as reassurance, loss, hope, joy, anticipation, acceptance, grief, longing, commitment, regret, revenge, and pride.

As you learn to scan songs for the core emotion driving them, you gain precious information about the craft-smart writers use to build an audience's interest in a song. Start using this critiquing system to mine information about your songs under construction.

Our first deep-dive critique is on "Chelsea Morning" by Joni Mitchell, one of the world's premier, iconic, and essential songwriters. While listening, write down on paper or in a computer document your answers to the questions in column A and B of the SAA Critiquing Tool #1.

Critiquing Exercise #1

"Chelsea Morning" ▸

by Joni Mitchell

> Woke up, it was a Chelsea morning, and the first thing that I heard
> Was a song outside my window, and the traffic wrote the words
> It came a-reeling up like Christmas bells, and rapping up like pipes and drums
> Oh, won't you stay
> We'll put on the day
> And we'll wear it 'till the night comes
>
> Woke up, it was a Chelsea morning, and the first thing that I saw
> Was the sun through yellow curtains, and a rainbow on the wall
> Blue, red, green and gold to welcome you, crimson crystal beads to beckon
>
> Oh, won't you stay
> We'll put on the day
> There's a sun show every second
>
> Now the curtain opens on a portrait of today
> And the streets are paved with passersby
> And pigeons fly
> And papers lie
> Waiting to blow away
>
> Woke up, it was a Chelsea morning, and the first thing that I knew
> There was milk and toast and honey and a bowl of oranges, too
> And the sun poured in like butterscotch and stuck to all my senses

Oh, won't you stay

We'll put on the day

And we'll talk in present tenses

When the curtain closes and the rainbow runs away

I will bring you incense owls by night

By candlelight

By jewel-light

If only you will stay

Pretty baby, won't you

Wake up, it's a Chelsea morning

Here's a brief critique of "Chelsea Morning," using Creative GPS.

⊙ Creative GPS Analysis of "Chelsea Morning"

Critique by author

🧠 Song Intention

She wants "What?" to happen by singing the song?

She wants to be desired, she wants the guy to stay.

😵 Core Emotion

What core emotion is driving the song?

Hope

🎵 Song Category

What song category does the song easily fall into?

New love

👥 Audience Tracking

What craft tools were used to get the audience to see their life in the song early in the writing process?

- *Repetition & Variation:* 1. using the title in the first line of each stanza/verse, creates repetition (memorability). 2. By swapping out just one word at the end of each stanza/verse (what she: heard, saw, knew) adds variation and an opportunity to write a visual response to what she heard, saw, and knew.

- *Summing Up:* She sums up the meaning of the stanza/verses with the lyric "Now the curtain opens on a portrait of today." The song has two bridges (two refrains) that lyrically "sum up" the visual pictures lyrically used in the verses/stanzas.

- *Harvesting Song DNA:* She uses images already in the song in a new context, "when the curtain closes and the rainbow runs away." She doesn't add new images, she reuses the images already in the song; a smart way to keep continuity and memorability going through out a song.

- *Using the word "you":* "Won't you stay." Change of perspective tied to song form: Singing to a general audience in one part of the song, then singing directly to the person the song is about in another heightens a song's urgency and the writers need to express emotion. This is a common strategy liberally used in good songwriting.

- The song has two bridges and *uses the timeline* of morning to night to harvest the song's intent to have him stay. The movement of time in songs is a strong audience tracking device. Here it's tied to song form; used effectively in the songs two bridges: "Now the curtain opens"—"When the curtain closes."

- *Rhyming:* The use of rhyming especially internal rhymes, adds to a song's memorability.

Critiquing Exercise #2

Use the Song Arts Academy critiquing tool to identify the intention, singular core emotion, and the mechanics driving the Script's "Breakeven."

Look for the use of original pictures and details when critiquing the song, so as to understand how song craft was applied in writing the song. You can also write a short "brief" explaining your critique. (See Opportunity Briefs and Premises in Part Two)

"Breakeven" ▸

by Andrew Frampton / Daniel O'Donoghue / Mark Sheehan / Stephen Kipner

> I'm still alive but I'm barely breathing
> Just prayed to a god that I don't believe in
> Cause I got time while she got freedom
> Cause when a heart breaks no it don't break even
>
> Her best days will be some of my worst
> She finally met a man that's gonna put her first
> While I'm wide awake she's no trouble sleeping
> Cause when a heart breaks no it don't break even, even no
>
> What am I supposed to do when the best part of me was always you?
> What am I supposed to say when I'm all choked up and you're ok?
> I'm falling to pieces, yeah I'm falling to pieces
>
> They say bad things happen for a reason
> But no wise words gonna stop the bleeding
> Cause she's moved on while I'm still grieving
> And when a heart breaks, no it don't break even, even, no

What am I gonna do when the best part of me was always you?

What am I supposed to say when I'm all choked up and you're ok?

I'm falling to pieces, yeah, I'm falling to pieces,

yeah I'm falling to pieces, I'm falling to pieces

You got his heart and my heart and none of the pain

You took your suitcase, I took the blame.

Now I'm try to make sense of what little remains

Cause you left with no love, with no love to my name.

I'm still alive but I'm barely breathing

Just prayed to a god that I don't believe in

Cause I got time while she got freedom

Cause when a heart breaks, no it don't break even

No it don't break, no it don't break even, no

What am I gonna do when the best part of me was always you?

What am I supposed to say when I'm all choked up and you're ok?

I'm falling to pieces, yeah, I'm falling to pieces,

yeah I'm falling to pieces, I'm falling to pieces

Oh, it don't break even, no Oh, it don't break even, no

📍 Creative GPS Analysis of "Breakeven"

🧠 Song Intention

The singer wants "What?" to happen by singing the song?

To come to terms, sort out a range of emotions from anguish to anger as he deals with a breakup, the end of a relationship.

😨 Core Emotion

What core emotions are driving the song?

Grief, loss, anger

🎵 Song Category

What song category does the song easily fall into?

Breakup song

👥 Audience Tracking

What craft tools were used to get the audience to see their life in the song early in the writing process?

- The audience knows it's a breakup song by the fourth line in the song; they don't have to hunt and peck to discover the reason the song is being sung.

- He reveals a remarkable trait about himself in the second stanza.

- He sings the first verse to a general audience.

- He sings the chorus directly to the girl, using the word "you" (as in, we are our favorite subject).

- There is a unique relationship between the songs lyric and melody keeping the audience deeply involved with the song. Can you tell what it is? Sad or dark lyric tied to happy/bright melody. Another well-used songwriting strategy that keeps audiences involved in songs.

Note to Readers about the Writing Prompts

The writing prompts in the *Elements* give readers an opportunity to use the craft tools introduced in each chapter. You can't make a mistake when writing your original song based on these prompts. Have fun, stretch, be creative, and, most importantly, don't stress over writing them.

With practice, the use of these craft tools will become second nature to you and your writing will benefit. Go for it!

Writing Prompt #1

Prompts 1a and 1b are designed to help practice visual storytelling tied to personal experiences and memories, by using descriptions more than statements.

Instructions:

Let the pictures and images tell the story in writing your song.

Circle around a few ideas, personal stories/experiences, and concepts before settling on the one you believe best to write the prompt about.

As you're considering what to write, ask yourself the same questions you did in the critique of "Chelsea Morning" and "Breakeven":

1. What core emotion is driving the creation of my song?

2. I'm singing my song because I want . . . ?

   - What's my intention in singing/writing it?

   - What do I want to have happen by writing the song?

   - What emotion do I want the audience to feel?

3. While your song is under construction:

Review the Song Mechanics™ list and apply it to your song under construction

Select one of the following two prompts to write:

Prompt 1a:

Write a song about someone in your past, someone you haven't seen in years, who at one time had a huge effect or influence on you for either good or bad.

What would you say to that person today if you had a chance to tell him or her what he or she meant to you, for better or worse?

Use objects and details, use your memories, set the time and place so we can see the place and time you're writing about.

Understand what you want to say about how the experience made you better or gave you challenges to overcome.

Keep it simple.

Circle around a few ideas before you settle on one. Understand clearly why you are writing the song and what purpose writing it serves. Know what the audience's takeaway will be.

Prompt 1b:

Write a song about a person who was either a stranger or a passing acquaintance that you used to see in your neighborhood all the time and now, for reasons unknown, one day you realize, you don't see him or her around anymore.

What may have happened to the person? What impression or feeling did he or she leave you with when you saw or interacted with him or her? Fear, regret, sadness, loathing, hope, reassurance, remorse?

The song should be as much about you as it is about the person. Let the audience know what was so compelling about the effect that person had on you that you wrote a song about him or her. What was at stake for you writing it!

It can be speculative or personal. Draw on your memories, impressions, and experiences.

Describe the story, the scene, the emotions stirred in you by person's face, body, and attitudes.

1. Who was that person?

2. What, if any, was your relationship to him or her?

3. What kind of reaction or feelings did the person cause you to have when you saw him or her?

4. Where could that person possibly be now?

5. How did he or she get there?

6. What's the difference between you and that person?

7. Explore the thoughts and feelings that flow from the curious serendipity of how yours and other people's lives and habits intersect.

8. How and why do good and/or terrible things happen? Speculate. Tell their story, your story. Tell a compelling story. The objective is to be descriptive, set the scene.

9. Think about songs that do this. Make a short list of songs you know that do this. My list includes Joni Mitchell's "For Free," the Hollies' "Bus Stop," the Beatles' "Eleanor Rigby," and Bob Dylan's "Like a Rolling Stone."

Developing Song Concepts

As mentioned in the introduction, concepts do the heavy lifting in songwriting: a good concept gets you half way or 50 percent to your goal; a great concept, 75 percent; and a brilliant one, 90 percent toward writing a song that has a chance to stand up and last.

Song craft tools are needed to build the remaining 50 percent 25 percent, and 10 percent of the song, but that's an easier job to do when the concept itself provides the basis for surprise, originality, honesty, inspiration, or flat-out entertainment value of the song.

Since audiences know so many songs, the pressure's naturally on songwriters to bring a fresh blend of "surprise and familiarity" to capture and keep an audience's attention.

The following ideation strategies offer ways to develop song concepts to fully engage each strand of opportunity inherent in the concept itself, your intention to write it, and the core emotion(s) driving the song. (To ensure it's built so an audience needs or wants to hear it.)

Good songs are written as a response to an event. What's the core reason motivating you to write about that event (your intention) and what song craft tools will you put to work to make the song memorable? (Creative GPS–Audience Tracking) Maximum song momentum; stickiness to an audience, is generated when a song's concept is married to "song form," using strategies that:

1. Invite audiences to "See their life" in the song, as well as by

2. Employing craft strategies that remove all impediments to momentum (deleting Empty Calorie Words, vetting notions, and a host of other editorial tools to be discussed). The removal of impediments allows "feeling to triumph over thinking," creating a state of Emotional Hypnotism in the listener.

Lyric and melodic development tied to song form is a critically important concept to grasp and execute. Much as how on-time trains arrive at each stop of their route on schedule, so too can a song's lyric and melody be written to arrive on time at key places in the song form. Writing with this knowledge builds intense torque and momentum throughout a song and keeps audiences invested in the song/on the train throughout its entire length.

Run your concepts, ideas, and titles through this select strategy guide and see which approaches pay creative dividends for a current song or developing title you're working on!

Sixteen Song Title Ideation Strategies

1. **The Genesis Line Strategy**™—Is where you come up with a title or write the whole song based on the inspiration generated from one line or song title. Examples: "Cake by the Ocean," "24 Carat Magic," "Our Love Is Here to Stay," "The Race is On," "Hella Good." This approach typically leads to the genesis line being used at the start and end of a chorus in the AABABCA song form, ("You've lost that loving feeling") or as the first and last line of a song, ("Yesterday") or as a "tagline" song. Where the title is "tagged" onto the last line of a chorus, verse, stanza, or refrain ("Cake by the Ocean"). Once you've settled on a song title, run it through the other strategies/see which provides the best avenue for self-expression and an audience's connection to the song.

2. **The Debate Team Strategy**™—Is where you weigh or debate a number of ways to write the idea, the song premise (based on the genesis line/song title) and choose which approach best suits the writer and the song. Sometimes this includes making the song a "story song" and all the benefits that storytelling offers to songwriters (including all the advantages that come from structuring a beginning, middle, and ending).

   Other times, we might debate the various or contrasting points of view available to write the song from. For example, the following titles could be written two ways:

   - Example One: "You're Gonna Need a Bigger Heart" can be written from a *universal space*: to ask people to give more of themselves to make the world a better place as the state of the world demands each of us care or do more to make the world a better place, or

   - Example Two: "I'm Gonna Need a Bigger Heart" can be written from a more *personal space*: the need for the singer or writer to make room in his or her own heart to forgive a friend or lover's transgression. Another example:

   - Example Three: Ariana Grande's "Problem" featuring Iggy Azalea. The song was a huge success the way it was written, but as an example, it could be written a few ways. The way "Problem" was written was using the title to say, 'I should leave you, I'd have one less problem without you if I did but I want you, so even though the relationship has gone bad, we're still hanging out.' This way it's a "disillusionment with love" song. That's valid for the song and audience it's aimed at.

- Example Four: "Problem" could also be written as an empowerment song by debating/writing the idea (genesis line) from the point of view of the woman actually ending the relationship and now, "I got one less problem without you," spells out she ended the relationship and is free of the problem and because of that decision, new, more promising opportunity has opened up!

3. **The Problem-Solution Setup**™—Is a technique for using a verse to illustrate a "Problem" then a chorus to illustrate the "Solution" to that problem. "You've Got a Friend" written by Carol King is a good example. This approach also works in reverse, whereby a chorus illustrates a problem (for example, how bad a breakup feels), with a verse contrasting/illustrating how good the relationship once was.

4. **The Environmental Strategy**—Is where all five senses are used to create visual images, storytelling/metaphors, similes, and analogies to write a song. For example, Joni Mitchell's "Chelsea Morning," "Both Sides Now," and Rodgers & Hammerstein's "My Favorite Things."

5. **The Vignette Strategy**—Is where each verse tells a different story or vignette connected by the chorus. Again, Joni Mitchell's "Both Sides Now" or Dawes's "A Little Bit of Everything," Ty Herndon's "A Man Holding on to a Woman Letting Go," Leonard Cohen's "Everybody Knows" are good examples of vignette strategies in action.

6. **Single-Word Titles**—Songs like "Help," "Belief," "Try," "Torn," etc. Owning a word, a name, or place as in a single-word title is a lofty goal for songwriters to aim for.

7. **Songs with "Action(s)" in Their Title**—"Living on a Prayer," "Working My Way Back to You," "If It's the Last Thing I Do," "Every Breath You Take."

8. **Songs with One Word Changed in Their Title**—"As Time Goes By"–"As Tears Go By"; "Rhythm of the Night"–"Rhythm of the Sun."

9. **Setups: Making Comparisons or Conclusions**—"Our Love Is Here to Stay": "In time the Rockies may crumble, Gibraltar may tumble, they're only made of clay, but our love is here to stay." "All of Me": "You took the part that once was my heart, so why not take all of me." Also, "Summertime Blues."

10. **The Tag Line Song**™---Is where the title is "tagged on" to the end of a verse or refrain. Examples include: Prince's "When Doves Cry," Billy Joel's "She's Always a Woman to Me," Bryan Adams's "Everything I Do," Chick Rains and Wade Hayes "Old Enough to Know Better," Bob Dylan's "Gates of Eden."

11. **The Sandwich**—Is where the title is used at the start of a stanza, verse, or chorus and is repeated at the end of a stanza, verse, or chorus. Songs such as "Yesterday," "I Fall to Pieces," "Where Is Love?" Alan Jackson's "I Don't Even Know Your Name."

12. **The Authority Song**™—Are songs where you sound like you know something no one else does. Songs such as Bob Dylan's "Like a Rolling Stone," or "The Times They Are A-Changin', Jimi Hendrix's "The Wind Cries Mary."

13. **The Reveal**—Is where the song has a lyrical emotional surprise, or twist. This is typically used in the tag line song format where the title is "tagged on" to the last line of a verse, stanza, or chorus. Songs with strong reveals include: Logic's "800-273-8255," in which the title is not even sung in the song, or Larry Boone, Paul Nelson, and Richie McDonald's "Everything's Changed," Performed by Lonestar, Hank Cochran's "Why Can't He Be You," Ray Davis's "Lola," Jamie O'Hara's "The Cold Hard Truth," Shel Silverstein's "A Boy Named Sue," Don Schlitz and Paul Overstreet's "When You Say Nothing At All." (performed by Keith Whitley and Alison Krauss).

14. **Novelty Titles**—Is taking places, events, famous characters from real life or fairy tales, stories, history, or mythology and finding ways to turn them into song titles, also double-entendres: "Every Cinderella Has Her Midnight," "Alice, This Ain't Wonderland," "Boys Lie, It's Something in Their Jeans," "I'm Victoria's Secret."

15. **Singing "Stream of Conscious"** words, syllables, and sounds to a melody line or track. This free association approach has yielded some very famous songs and is used by many successful songwriters.

16. **Mirror Writing Strategies**—Writing original lyrics to the rhythm and rhyme scheme of a well-known song, then creating an original melody and chord pattern to match the mirror written lyrics. Writing an original melody and lyric over a preexisting set of chord changes.

2
Making Distinctions
Songs under Construction

Harvesting Song DNA

Intention is the three clicks of Dorothy's ruby red slippers! Knowing your intention, the reason you're writing a song, always brings you home.

Just as indigenous peoples harvest every part of an animal, leaving nothing unused, so too should good songwriters harvest every part of their musical and lyrical ideas. The very nature of a good idea offers many ways to write it; that's what makes it good. Developing a song's potential, seeing the opportunity of what can be written or implied by its title, is one of the most satisfying aha moments of discovery for songwriters.

If we take Joni Mitchell's "Chelsea Morning" as an example of good song harvesting, we can see how she stays inside the song's DNA to harvest its full potential.

We follow her from morning to evening. The morning perhaps symbolizes the newness of a relationship and/or a promise of the unfolding day and the hope that a relationship might flourish. The harvest is poetically expressed by the enlivened new feelings of love that transform the everyday world around her so that:

- The traffic wrote the words and

- The sun poured in like butterscotch . . .

It's a love song that never uses the word *love* in it, it doesn't have to; the joy in the melody expresses it.

The strength of a song's idea can be determined by how many strands of opportunity are fully harvested throughout its form and also by the masterful use of song craft. In this case, Ms. Mitchell:

- Anchored the entire song with a *Genesis Line* at the start of each verse: "Woke up it was a Chelsea Morning and the first thing that I _____"

- Used a *Vignette Strategy* to swap out one word at the end of each verse for what she *heard, saw, and knew* (a great use of repetition and variation)

- Then, told us exactly what she heard, saw, and knew (using an *Environmental Strategy* to put all the details of her environment into the song to harvest them)

- Used two bridges (or refrains) to sum up her logic by telling us "Why" she wrote what she wrote: in bridge one by saying: "Now the curtain opens on a portrait of today," and in bridge two: "When the curtain closes and the rainbow runs away"

The construction of these evocative images and the craft that forged them are a treasure trove for Songwriting Athletes to study and learn how to harvest song DNA and then apply that knowledge in their next song.

The seamless simplicity, directness, logic, poetry, and elegance of every songwriting decision creates hypnosis in the service of new love here.

Another way to think of harvesting your idea's potential is to understand that each lyric and melodic line you write is either adding momentum or drag to your song.

Figure out the logic, the "Why?" of each lyric line in your song, how it connects to or clarifies the previous line as well as sets up the next line.

The same is true with melody. Is your melody building on the previous sung melodic line? Is it adding variation rhythmically (or dynamic contrast)? Is it moving slightly higher in the register at key points in the song development? These are all good signs of momentum.

Look to continually spell out your song's DNA code, the full potential of your idea and its root concept as your song moves forward.

Vetting Notions

An idea by itself is not enough. Good songs are written as a response to an event. As simple as that sounds, it's profound. Many developing writers mistakenly believe their ideas are gaining traction, landing with a one-two punch, when in fact they merely point to a series of details about an event. A deeper connection to the song's essence, its DNA, is not made clear. This communication breach is called a notion.

Make a distinction between fully harvested ideas for songs and notions for songs.

Notions point toward or suggest connections; they don't actually make connections between the writer's intention and the audience's understanding of it.

When writers are certain that their song's message is clear and concise, but the meaning remains unclear to the audience, that's a sign of that the song is still in the notion stage.

Fully harvested ideas have destinations. Each line builds its case for the reason it is written and sung; the lines have interior logic. As a result, audiences instantly grasp why they're listening; there's no excessive hunting and pecking for meaning.

Developing writers can easily believe the passion for their idea is magically translating to an audience understanding when, more often than not, the lyric is too vague for an audience to connect with it.

Although good ideas can start as notions, you need to hold your songwriting to high standards of clarity. You and your audience will be better served by choosing stronger concepts and ideas and then writing them with clear intent.

To Inspire or Entertain

Most songs are designed to accomplish one of two goals: to inspire or entertain. Of course, a song can do both.

Knowing which goal your song aims to achieve early in the writing process frames many important decisions, including who your audience is and what emotional tone, the setting of music, melody, arrangement, or track will be most effective to communicate your intention.

When listening to songs, get in the habit of asking yourself whether it's an inspiration- or entertainment-based song.

Listening this way peels away another layer of mystery about why songs work emotionally on audiences. Let this be a factor in deciding what ideas and assets to include in your songs.

What to Leave In, What to Leave Out

A journalist once asked Elmore Leonard, the famed author of *Hombre*, *Get Shorty*, and many others, why people loved his books so much. He answered, "Because I leave out everything people don't want to read."

Can you leave out everything people don't want to hear?

Can you make a distinction between what needs or doesn't need to be said lyrically and musically in your songs? Let your intention, the rails keeping songs on track moving forward, be the deciding factor.

As the writer, you're the first audience member and editor, the Rembrandt choosing where to throw the light. You decide who or what subjects to highlight, what to regard or disregard, what essence or message is really at the heart of your song. What you don't say matters as much as what you do in songwriting. So, how does one develop this sense of positive and negative space in a song?

Invitations

A few principles can help decide what stays and goes. One principle is choosing to invite a larger audience into our songs by how we write a line.

Let's take a section of the Beatles' "Yesterday" as an example. If you look at the first and second lines of the bridge (the line ending with the word "say"), notice that it is written as "open-ended," meaning anyone can relate to it.

If the line was written:

> *"Why she had to go, I told her no, her mother couldn't stay"*

That's closed; it's great for the 8 percent of audiences who have mother-in-law issues, but kills the invitation to the other 92 percent of audience to enter the song.

Starting Songs Deeper into Their Story

Another editorial approach is *starting your song deeper into the story line* so the listener is taken by surprise and starts paying greater attention at once.

This technique is like what happens when overhearing a disagreement between a couple an aisle over in a supermarket; your natural curiosity to know what the argument is about sharpens your listening for details . . .

The Script used this technique in the opening lines of "Breakeven":

> *"I'm still alive but I'm barely breathing,*
> *Just prayed to a god that I don't believe in"*

We don't know what these lyrics mean or what they are in service of until they add the next two lines, but they got our attention by starting the song in the middle of the singers anguish.

The No-Setup Song

Often we think a song needs more setting up that it does. Songs thrive in a simply and urgent environment. Long, drawn-out additions of music or lyrics are unnecessary information killing the hypnosis process. Songs can be overly set up via:

- Long musical intros

- 16-bar verses that can be cut to 8 or 4

- 8-bar prechoruses that can be cut to 4 or 2

- Double choruses where single will do

- Removing the pre in the second verse

- Overlong solo or solo sections at all

Choruses pay off by making smart early economical lyrical and form decisions.

Leave out unnecessary notes and words.

Write so an audience "Sees their life" in your song. Orchestrating the use of very specific and general information in songwriting can be challenging. A few factors play a role in deciding where or when specific and general details get used in songs, including who is the audience aimed at or the particular philosophies of writing partners.

Keep in mind writing the environment around you (the use of unique pictures and images) or tapping into emotions and details of everyday life, the use of time as a factor of urgency, or the use of objects to tell a story in your songwriting.

The use of these components create a heady lyrical mix of richness, color, empathy, originality, and style and should be liberally used in creating well-written songs.

3

Balancing Acts: Creative Clarity/Editorial Tools
Using Lyrical Grammar

We've established we're in the communications business. What we're communicating is our intention. By writing songs around a core emotion, we have a weathervane to point to and distinguish which words and concepts support our intention and the song's core emotion(s) and which do not.

Making these three distinctions early builds the song's foundation.

Song form is so short that getting anything wrong early creates problems later in building a good song. Each writing decision; our intention, song topic, emotion, song category, melody, use of repetition, and so on matter in having a shot at writing songs that last and stand up over time.

Just as Manhattan real estate is insanely expensive, so too is the *real estate value* of every word, line, and note you choose. Each is either adding to or subtracting from your song's momentum. (A great song idea is Midtown; a notion or bad idea, a graveyard in an outer borough.)

Songs serve two muses: Creativity (imagination/ingenuity) and Clarity (discipline). Great songs get this balance completely correct. If you skew the scale to favor one over the other, a song's potential starts to suffer.

When developing writers overtly favor imagination over discipline, clarity can suffer. This leads to the hypnosis process stopping cold.

With all the jobs good songwriters need to do, writing with clarity so an audience sees their life in the song is high on the list.

Developing songwriters can be so certain their intention is crystal clear and their lyrics exceedingly well written, but the audience's reaction decides the reality of how well written songs are, not the writer.

When meaning is unclear, the audience does not know who to root for or why the song, story, or emotion should matter to them. After a short period of listening without connecting these emotional dots, they metaphorically look at their watch, tune out, and move on underwhelmed . . .

As said prior but worth repeating, developing writers need to closely watch this line between where it feels so good to write a song, and the reality of how good the song actually is. *Standards matter and standards equal clarity.*

Lyrical Grammar is an umbrella term for six editorial tools, defined as

- Shrink Wrapping

- Empty Calorie Words

- Summing Up

- Clarifying Statements

- Calculating Distance to Target, and

- Lyrical Logic

These tools help writers make critical distinctions in balancing creativity and clarity, and sharpen perception about which songwriting decisions keep audiences deeply involved in a song lyric.

Let's review them here:

Shrink Wrapping

Shrink Wrapping helps writers ultimately define what stays in or what is ultimately removed from a song's lyric or melody. (For melody, see chapter on melodic studies.) There are a few moving parts:

Lyrically, it's the process of moving the most important details, images, concepts, and statements up from the middle or back of a song to the front, giving a song significant momentum early.

It's also the process of zooming in on *your intention*, so less relevant details of a lyric are removed so the essential interior details may flourish.

So much information seems needed when we begin writing to get the song rolling, but once a first draft is completed, we can begin rewriting by Shrink Wrapping.

Shrink Wrapping a Lyric Written Too Wide

When a lyric is written too wide, its message is too general, its detail unspecific; this causes the song to suffer a loss of momentum and engagement.

Lyrics written too wide lack uniqueness, causing audiences to lose interest.

Here's an example of a line written too wide:

> *"I know you're in pain, you're hurt*
> *and you think I judge you, not true*
> *I'm not, it's a thing you do,*
> *I'm a friend who cares*
> *and only wants to help see you through."*

That's wide: too general, not descriptive, no color or pictures, and all statements.

Yes, the line gives us information, but not in a memorable or unique way. The use of pictures, images, on the other hand, are sticky.

The same sentiment shrink wrapped can be written:

> *"I'm not pointing a finger, I'm reaching out a hand."*

It takes ten words in the shrink-wrapped example as opposed to the thirty-one words in the written "wide" example.

Shrink Wrapping a lyric by turning statements into pictures takes practice, but well worth the effort to develop the practice.

Empty Calorie Words™

Empty Calorie Words are words used often in songs but that by nature are too general and nondescriptive. Words like *this, thing, something, it's, love, and pain* are examples of Empty Calorie Words.

Developing writers use them liberally, falsely trusting they represent more meaning than they actually do. These words "point to meaning" as a suggestive form of shorthand, but fail to add much surprise, color, or momentum essential to writing original songs.

Developing writers should be skeptical when they see them enter their lyrics.

A productive response to them is to ask yourself; "What kind of pain? What kind of love? What 'thing' am I writing about?" Work a little harder/dig a little deeper creatively to answer those questions by coming up with a lyric line more descriptive in detail and originality.

As small a fix as the following example represents, when applied to three or six lines in a song, the removal of Empty Calorie Words makes for more personal, descriptive, and nuanced writing:

> "We can't repair *this* broken dream"

> "We can't repair *our* broken dream"

Shrink Wrapping and the removal of Empty Calorie Words applied across an entire song leads to shortening verses, prechorus, choruses, and bridges/refrains.

Rethinking what was initially thought to need four lines can be better said in two, or those eight lines of lyrics can be shrink wrapped to four. Much like a puzzle piece on the bottom can't move into an adjacent spot until another piece moves above it.

Shrink Wrapping also applies to our Intention. For example, if you wrote about a breakup, you might think the song's about your justified anger at discovering the lies you were told that lead to the breakup. Filling up the entire song with anger at the discovery might be only one important part of the story.

The song may actually be about a deeper subject; the feeling of abandonment. Perhaps a pattern of abandonment in many prior relationships. That deeper story, if true, is rich for harvesting and leads to a deeper reveal of honesty, a need to write and thereby a need for an audience to connect.

The editorial beauty of Shrink Wrapping opens the rest of the song form to the rich relevant veins of emotion and storytelling present in the opportunity to write your song.

It takes experience; writing a lot of songs, to get the balance of what to leave in and what to leave out just right. Gain it by making every note and every word fight for its right to exist in your songs!

Summing Up

It makes logical sense to frame the conversation you're having with the listener by putting context to it before moving on or adding new information. That's what Summing Up is.

Summing Up is literally the writing of two lines of lyrics to clarify why you wrote the previous lines and is tied to song form.

An example of summing up is used in the first prechorus of Ed Sheeran and Amy Hodges's "Thinking Out Loud."

Verse one:

1. When your legs don't work like they used to before

2. And I can't sweep you off of your feet

3. Will your mouth still remember the taste of my love?

4. Will your eyes still smile from your cheeks?

Prechorus one:

5. And, darling, I will be loving you 'til we're 70

6. And, baby, my heart could still fall as hard at 23

Lines 1 through 4 use images/pictures to start the story and draw us into the song. (Pictures are sticky/memorable.)

Lines 5 and 6 *sum up* or spell out in a statement exactly what they meant by writing lines 1 through 4.

The meaning/intention is not left to interpretation. Age is the driving factor in writing these lines that show commitment.

Summing Up is a smart use of **Creative Clarity**, letting a writer fully harvest an idea or intention before moving on to add a new idea or line to the song.

For developing writers, as you're learning to see opportunities in songs to sum up, consciously be on the lookout for how many individual lines you've written (typically 4–6) where you haven't summed up yet!

In these lines, you have not made clear why you sang/wrote the preceding lines. (The bridge or refrain in a song is the *ultimate* Summing Up position in songs.

The rule of thumb to know when to sum up is to ask ourselves or our imaginary audience, "Hey, audience, if you want to know *why* I just wrote these four lines, I'm gonna spell it out clearly for you right here in these next two lines."

Clarifying Statements

An example of a Clarifying Statement is in Joni Mitchell's refrain(s) of "Chelsea Morning":

> Woke up, it was a Chelsea morning,
> and the first thing that I saw
> Was the sun through yellow curtains,
> and a rainbow on the wall
> Blue, red, green and gold to welcome you,
> crimson crystal beads to beckon
>
> Oh, won't you stay
> We'll put on the day
> There's a sun show every second

Clarifying Statement:

> Now the curtain opens on a portrait of today
> And the streets are paved with passersby
> And pigeons fly
> And papers lie
> Waiting to blow away

By writing, "Now the curtain opens on a portrait of today," Mitchell clarifies the use of all the verse images. It frames them, harvests them, connects them to the verse, so she can move onto what else needs to be said in the song.

Calculating Distance to Target

This is a strategy used early in the development of a song concept, lyric, or title. It ties the strength of ideas inherent in a songs concept to specific lines/places in the song form.

Certain parts or lines in the **Song Form** *offer more important opportunities to build lyric and musical momentum*, thereby are **Targeted** early in the writing process.

These key lines or parts are typically:

- The first two lines of a verse

- The last line of a prechorus

- The first and last lines of a chorus (the song title placement)

- And the first line of a second verse

Lyrical Logic

Lyrical Logic is writing an *image followed by a statement* to clarify why the image was used. For example:

> "If you've got a halo don't let it shine too bright" (Image)

> "I'm not looking for good tonight" (Statement)

or

> "That hill is now an on ramp to an interstate" (Image)

> "Time puts its stamp on all things in its wake" *(Statement)*

Writing with this perspective enables writers to harvest and metabolize ideas before adding new ones.

Lyrical Grammar and Song Form

A writer can maximize the use of Lyrical Grammar tools by tying it to song form.

Hundreds of thousands of years of people listening to songs have hardwired song form into human beings; we know when the chorus is coming or an introduction is ending and a verse is starting. That, and when a prechorus is ending leading us back to a chorus, then to a bridge or refrain.

Smart, experienced writers know and take advantage of song form power when building their songs.

Although every line in a song is important, some are more so based on where those lines fall in the song form.

For example, the opening two lines of a song need to grab the listener's attention.

The next two lines, perhaps to give a clue of what the song's about and why the singer is singing it.

The first line of a prechorus can sum up the verse (point back to why you said what you said in the verse). And the last line of a prechorus to "set up" (why you'll say the first line or song title line in the downbeat or tag of the chorus).

Using song forms of AABA, AABCACB, or ABAB may create variations or different opportunities to sum up but the key takeaway is Lyrical Grammar exists and using it makes for effective communication.

Experienced producers, publishers, writers, or collaborators can look at a lyric sheet and know in an instant whether the songwriter knows this critical info or does not. It adds momentum if you do, or wastes precious time and drag if you don't, much like how downhill racers or professional drivers cut fractions of seconds off each turn or curve as they know how to enter each just right.

Use these editorial tools in the next ten to thirty songs you write and see the level of creative clarity and growth you achieve by making these distinctions.

Free Association Songs

While we're on the subject of clarity and editing, there are popular styles of songwriting where clarity is not the driving force behind making a song great and yet they are magnificent creations loved by millions and for good reason. I call them Free Association songs.

Free association songs are like Rorschach tests; their lyrics are free-form and designed to float in our conscious much like clouds suggesting shapes in a sky. When they're great, they are unique gems of artistic creation. One of my favorite Free association songs is "A Whiter Shade of Pale." (And most every song by Procol Harum.) "The Walrus" and "Me and My Arrow" are other examples. A favorite free association songwriter is Jillette Johnson. Her songs wind along, gaining momentum and meaning; she's gifted and original in her language, images, and moods she creates.

It's only one opinion, but typically a very small percentage of free association writers achieve the alchemy of high art, and it's very easy for developing writers to fall into the free association song mode and think they are making high art.

I suggest developing writers are best served long term by learning the ins and outs of intention-based writing for the simple reason it gives writers lots of specific tools to ground them in practicing song craft.

Take for example John Lennon, one of songwriting's best intention-based writers. Songs like "In My Life," "Help!" and "A Hard Day's Night," are gems representing just a small percentage of his outstanding intention-based songwriting. He got those skills together first, long before writing free association songs, such as "The Walrus," 'Strawberry Fields," or "Lucy in the Sky with Diamonds," songs where intention doesn't play much of a role outside of having fun playing with mood, images, textures, and language. He also came back from a love of writing free association songs to write one of the all-time great intention-based songs of his time: "Imagine."

Learning to put the editorial tools of Lyrical Grammar to use in intention-based writing gives writers extremely clear sight lines to decide what stays or goes in building songs that serve core emotions.

Gain mastery in thinking this way. Learn first to be a clarity rock star! That's a smart goal for developing songwriters: to get the balance of creativity and clarity just right in the next fifteen to twenty five songs you write, then, if or when you write a free association song, great, it will be by choice.

4
Identifying Song Categories and Core Emotions

One of the four parts (or vectors) of Creative GPS introduced prior is knowing what category the song your writing falls into.

Just as song form is hardwired into listeners, so too are song categories. Audiences innately know devotional love songs, new love, breakup songs, makeup songs, party songs, anthems, coming of age, or songs of reassurance. When well written, they signal the listener to organically connect their experiences to them.

Adding to the SAA Critiquing System, let's tie each song category to one or more core emotions that drive(s) them. Here's a short list of general song categories (not all), and the corresponding emotion(s) (not all) we typically look to evoke in a listener:

Song Category	Core Emotion
Relationship Songs:	
Devotional love	Commitment
New love	Hope
Disillusionment love	Confusion, anger, frustration, longing
Unrequited love	Loss, rejection, disillusionment, regret, revenge
Makeup	Forgiveness, regret, hope, relief
Breakup	Loss, grief, regret, rejection, acceptance
Coming to terms with love	Uncertainty
Coming-of-age	Freedom, disillusionment
Attitude	Swagger, party, sex, anger, frustration, revenge, revolution, challenge authority, fun
Empowerment	Control
Optimism	Freedom, positivity

Anthems	Various; e.g., empowerment
Reassurance	Comfort
Alienation	Longing, anger, hope, frustration, confusion

Knowing the song category and the core emotion that drives it helps writers make smart decisions about the song they're building early. Decisions like:

- What stories, ideas, and lyrics support the emotion and which do not (select or dismiss)

- Creating emotional contrast using the verse-chorus structure; The Problem-Solution Setup, e.g., in a breakup song, show the good times (in the verse), then show the bad times, problem (in the chorus).

- Allowing the use of time as a factor creating urgency in the song. The present, the past, and the future are powerful perspective choices ratcheting up the urgency or need to sing the song itself.

What business are we songwriters in? Yes, that's right, the communication business!

When these decisions show up in your writing, it shouts out to friends, family, colleagues, and music industry gatekeepers that you know you're in the communications business.

Part of being a good communicator is aiming at the right audience. A strong case could be made that the list of song categories above could account for up to 75 to 80 percent of all song topics typically heard in popular songs.

It's important to note that each category of song I've listed (these nests, so to speak) have been built many times before by countless generations of songwriters preceding us.

There's so much to learn from studying your favorite songs in each topic category, so apply the critiquing skills you're acquiring here to studying them and unlock their inner workings.

Pop the hood, gaze into the internal workings of your favorite songs, marvel at how they're built, then apply your new knowledge to your latest song! The critiquing tools in this book are designed exactly for that purpose.

Interestingly, song form, syncopation, slang, vocabulary, instrumentation, musical production methods, and styles change radically over time. The subjects and emotions people care about do not.

Your stories and unique personal details are part of your journey through loss, hope, rejection, commitment, grief, forgiveness, control, and comfort. Use them; they are the gemstones of your experience: they add sparkle, color, and originality to familiar topics.

The following song categories are old and have history, but the way you write the details of your experience are made new with each generation. It's a powerful reminder that good songs are a combination of the familiar and the surprising, so aim to surprise!

The Devotional Love Song

Devotional love songs perfectly illustrate the variety, honesty, and simplicity of good songwriting. Make a list and analyze five devotional love songs that have made an impression on you. You'll discover many devotional love songs are interesting, complex, and rich.

Yes, love is universal, but the details, habits, and qualities of each individual are unique.

The pledge: "I'm Yours," "(Everything I Do) I Do It for You"

The promise: "I Swear"

Overcome an obstacle: "Ain't No Mountain High Enough," "No Place That Far"

The statement that life sucks without you: "How Can I Live without You," "Without You"

The statement that something lost, found, taken for granted, discovered, or rediscovered was due to a lover: "Now That I Found You"

The statement that life is awesome with you in it: "I've Had the Time of My Life," "Perfect Day"

Critiquing Exercise #3: "Thinking Out Loud"

Use the craft tools outlined in this and previous chapters to critique Ed Sheeran and Amy Hodges's song "Thinking Out Loud."

Song Craft Review List

1. Make an analysis of the song, using Creative GPS and the SAA Critiquing Tool #1

2. Notice where in the song the following craft tools are used:

    - Creative Clarity

    - Lyrical Grammar: Summing Up—Clarifying Statements—Lyrical Logic

    - Lyrical Grammar tied to song form

    - Identifying the song category and its related core emotion

    - How many hooks are in the song

    - How the melody builds through the song form

    - Recognize when, how, and why in the song the writer uses original metaphors, similes, images, and personal details.

    - Recognize what the writer's Intention is in singing the song. What emotional response does he or she want the listener to have?

    - What other Audience Tracking tools are being use to keep the audience involved in the song?

"Thinking Out Loud" ▶

by Ed Sheeran and Amy Wadge

> When your legs don't work like they used to before
> And I can't sweep you off of your feet
> Will your mouth still remember the taste of my love?
> Will your eyes still smile from your cheeks?

And, darling, I will be loving you 'til we're 70

And, baby, my heart could still fall as hard at 23

And I'm thinking 'bout how people fall in love in mysterious ways

Maybe just the touch of a hand

Well, me—I fall in love with you every single day

And I just wanna tell you I am

(CHORUS)

So honey now

Take me into your loving arms

Kiss me under the light of a thousand stars

Place your head on my beating heart

I'm thinking out loud

That maybe we found love right where we are

When my hair's all but gone and my memory fades

And the crowds don't remember my name

When my hands don't play the strings the same way

I know you will still love me the same

'Cause honey your soul could never grow old, it's evergreen

And, baby, your smile's forever in my mind and memory

I'm thinking 'bout how people fall in love in mysterious ways

Maybe it's all part of a plan

Well, I'll just keep on making the same mistakes

Hoping that you'll understand

Coming-of-Age Songs

Coming-of-age songs explore the challenges of growing up: navigating new demands, leaving old frames of reference behind, new initiations. They are rich fishing ground for song topics that connect with a huge audience. A few I love: "Fast Car," "Strawberry Wine," "Closer to Fine," "She's Leaving Home," "Suds in the Bucket."

Critiquing Exercise #4: "Coast"

Use the craft tools outlined in this and previous chapters, including and the Song Craft Review List, to critique Billy Seidman and Brent Anderson's song "Coast."

"Coast" ▶

by Billy Seidman and Brent Anderson

>A Saturday morning summer day
>That hilltop seemed so far away
>We pedaled so hard our bodies swayed
>Sarah, Ann, and me
>
>Sarah was smart, n' Annie was cool
>My best friends from middle school
>Riding our bikes an' headed to
>Our favorite place to be
>
>We'd get so out of breath, still we never stopped
>We'd work up such a sweat, but once we reached the top, we'd
>
>(CHORUS)
>Coast, the thing we loved the most
>When life and time stood still
>Flying down that endless hill
>Streamers snappin' in the wind
>Friends maxing' out their Schwinns

I'd be the last to win, to pass that milepost

Cause I just loved to coast

Now twenty-two is not thirteen

Reality can really crowd your dreams

This commuter train rocks and screams

As I ride to work each day

The only breeze I ever seem to get

Is my boss breathing down my neck

Most mornings I'm a wreck

In a caffeinated haze

No time to drift or dream or talk to my old friends

Bet they're wishing just like me they could go back home again, and

(CHORUS)

(BRIDGE)

That hill is now an on ramp to an interstate

Time leaves it stamp on all things in its wake

Seems growing up's another hill to climb

Umm, just wish that I could find the time to coast

(LAST CHORUS)

My streamers snappin in the wind

My friends maxin' out their Schwinns

Aw, I'd let em win, they'd laugh n' call me toast,

But I just loved to coast, I just love to coast

I wish that I could coast

To listen to "Coast" go to: https://www.broadjam.com/songs/billyseidman/coast

Attitude Songs

Attitude songs need to swagger, swell, taunt, brag, tease, bitch intelligently or sarcastically, rebel, defy, be sexy. We're talking about up-tempo songs, party songs, Songs with infectious beats.

Strong, outrageous, fantasy-based songs. Powerful, confident songs. Songs that show off, that might even complain about something or someone. These songs are fun to write because they're simple; stick to one theme, add a few variations, and *boom*, you're on your way . . .

You don't get complicated with them. In classic rock, the Rolling Stones are masters of the attitude song.

Such songs as "19th Nervous Breakdown," "The Last Time," "Satisfaction," "Get Off of My Cloud," "Honky Tonk Women." Bruno Mars and Maroon 5 are also artists with deep discographies of attitude songs. The list of artists and songs that relish in attitude songs goes on and on.

Make a list of your favorite attitude songs. Ask yourself why they work for you. Remember, learning how to be a better writer is about ID'ing what you like and why you like it.

Train your instincts to *be on the lookout for cool word combinations and titles* and add them to your song title list.

You've got an advantage with these songs Music can matter more than words. These songs are feeling-driven. Other musical ingredients contributing:

1. Bass lines

2. Motifs-riffs

3. Call and answer

4. Smart use of song form

5. Use of repetition

Critiquing Exercise #5: Wake Up Call"

Use the craft tools outlined in all chapters and the Song Craft Review List (page TK) to critique the Maroon 5 song "Wake Up Call."

"Wake Up Call" ▶

by Adam Levine / James B. Valentine—Maroon 5

> I didn't hear what you were saying
> I live on raw emotion, baby
> I answer questions, never maybe
> And I'm not kind if you betray me
> So who the hell are you to save me?
>
> I never would've made it, baby
> If you needed love, well then ask for love
> Could've given love, now I'm taking love
> And it's not my fault, cause you both deserve
> What's coming now, so don't say a word
>
> (CHORUS)
> Wake up call, caught you in the morning
> With another one in my bed
> Don't you care about me anymore?
> Don't you care about me?
> I don't think so
> Six foot tall, came without a warning
> So I had to shoot him dead
> He won't come around here anymore
> Come around here,
> I don't think so

I would've bled to make you happy

You didn't need to treat me that way

And now you've beat me at my own game

And now I found you sleeping sound

And now your love is screaming loudly

I hear a sound and hit the ground

(CHORUS)

I don't feel so bad I don't feel so bad

(BRIDGE)

I'm so sorry, darling Did I do the wrong thing?

Oh, what was I thinking? Is his heart still beating?

(CHORUS)

Reassurance Songs

The major point in using song categories as a reference for song creation is to put your developing song on a collision course with millions of hearts/listeners.

People want to express devotion, or a longing for a simpler time in life, that or pull out all the entertainment stops in an attitude song. Another song category aimed at millions of people's hearts are reassurance songs.

Who doesn't need reassurance from time to time? It's a smart idea to use reassurance as a core emotion and category for your next song.

Bill Withers's "Lean on Me," Ben E. King's "Stand by Me," and Bob Marley's "Three Little Birds" are good examples.

Use the craft tools outlined in this and previous chapters, including the Song Craft Review List, to critique Paul Simon's masterpiece of reassurance "Bridge over Troubled Water."

Critiquing Exercise #6
"Bridge over Troubled Water"

"Bridge over Troubled Water" ▶

by Paul Simon

When you're weary, feeling small

When tears are in your eyes, I'll dry them all (all)

I'm on your side, oh, when times get rough

And friends just can't be found

Like a bridge over troubled water

I will lay me down

Like a bridge over troubled water

I will lay me down

When you're down and out

When you're on the street

When evening falls so hard

I will comfort you (ooo)

I'll take your part, oh, when darkness comes

And pain is all around

Like a bridge over troubled water

I will lay me down

Like a bridge over troubled water

I will lay me down

Sail on silver girl

Sail on by

Your time has come to shine

All your dreams are on their way

See how they shine

Oh, if you need a friend

I'm sailing right behind

Like a bridge over troubled water

I will ease your mind

Like a bridge over troubled water

I will ease your mind

Critique these or other favorite songs as the mood strikes:

- Empowerment songs: "Brave," "Roar," "Wide Awake"

- Breakup songs: "Wrecking Ball," "Try," "When I Was Your Man"

Writing Prompt #2

Your choice: write a devotional love song, a coming-of-age song, an attitude song, or a song of reassurance!

Use all the craft tools introduced to you in chapters 1, 2, and 3 to write your song.

Use the core emotion that drives the song category you write in, to drive the song category you've chosen.

Say something *urgent*.

Connect with your need, interest, or intent to write the song. Make sure your song has a finish line (what you want to have happen by writing it). Ensure that the reason you wrote it is clear to a listener.

- Lyrically: Use as many unique, but relatable, images to describe the situation in pictures.

  Show it, don't tell it. Make sure your lyrics sound the way people actually talk to each other. Make sure to balance your statements with pictures and your pictures with statements.

- Stretch! Circle around a few ideas, concepts, and situations until you settle on one that's radioactive for you to write, one that is urgent. Make sure you know exactly why it's a good or important idea for you to write and why other people will find it entertaining or inspiring to hear!

- Real estate: Remember every line in your song is extremely valuable real estate, how are you using your opening line? Those first lines are like the entrance on to a concert or theatrical stage. How are you getting our attention? How are you keeping it?

- How soon do we know what the song is about? What is it in service of?

This writing prompt exercise is designed for you to build songwriting muscle-perception. Have fun with it! You can't make a mistake!

Use Creative Clarity: Be clear and know the key emotion, the power plant emotion, driving your song. Check to make sure you're writing honest, image-driven lyrics, line by line, that develop and support your idea/story.

Are you adding momentum in each line? Is the line serving or distracting from your intent?

Exercise Emotional Hypnotism: Use the alchemy of images, details, and statements to consciously and unconsciously draw your audience deeper into your song, revealing their life in it.

Turn your *need* for writing the song into the fire that catches the listener's ear.

Be tough on yourself: Review and rewrite lines that are redundant, then "shrink-wrap" the lyric—speed up your storytelling. For example, if it's a love song, it's obvious; you don't need to use the word *love* much in the song. We all know it's about love. Instead, concentrate on what kind of love. What's at stake for you in keeping this love? In losing it? What are the details/images that spell out keeping or losing it?

The point in this assignment is to sharpen your song craft skills. If you're having a lot of aha moments, great! You're making better distinctions about what's going to best serve your song.

You're aiming and calibrating your shots with more refined criteria for what's brilliant, great, good, and okay.

Song Critique Checklist

1. Creative GPS Tools and Song DNA Harvesting

   - Apply all four components of Creative GPS when reviewing how successful a song's *Intention*, *Core Emotion*, and *Song Category* has been communicated, written, and harvested.

   - Note which *Audience Tracking* "Advanced Song Craft Tools" were used in writing the song.

   - Note what other Advanced Song Craft Tools or Ideation Strategies might also have been used to write it.

   - Note where the writer "harvested the song's DNA or Song Title" throughout the song or missed opportunities to do so.

2. Communication: Balancing Creativity with Clarity

   - On a scale from 1 to 10 (10 being the high score), how successful is the song's balance of Creativity to Clarity (*Surprise* to *Familiarity*)?

   - Where in the song form (or at which lines) did you have to "think" what the song was about?

   - Where in the song form (or at which lines) did you "feel" or "know" what the song was about?

   - How well has the writer balanced the use of *relatable* images, pictures, or metaphors to outright statements?

3. Use of Lyrical Grammar and Editorial Tools

   - When reading a song lyric, where do you notice in the lyric the writer used Lyrical Editorial Tools to write the song concisely?

   - What other Lyrical Grammar and Editorial Tools could have been used in writing the song?

4. Song Form: Melodic and Lyrical Development

- How well has the writer tied the song's melodic and lyrical development to the song form?

- Does the song's melody keep rising higher throughout the song form climaxing at the chorus?

- Is there unique, memorable, "hooky" melodic contrast in the song? How is the combination of step, rhythmic, and intervalic melodic motion used in the song tied to the song form?

5

Opportunity, Perspective, Momentum, and Contrast

Chapters 3 and 4 added Creative Clarity, Lyrical Grammar, and song categories to an essential list of songwriting tools. This chapter looks at the opportunity writing a song itself creates, how to harvest that opportunity using various perspective approaches, then harnessing momentum and contrast (both musical and lyrical) to shape a song's arc and sustainability.

A song of stunning conceptual power and execution is stealthy.

Deconstructing it's an afterthought as we're too enthralled experiencing the song in the moment to measure or critique it. (Another musical parallel to physics: the Heisenberg Uncertainty Principle!)

As students of song we must circle back, pop the hood, and take a closer look at the engine components to unmask the stealth driving a towering work of art.

Opportunity, perspective, momentum, and contrast (OPMC) are advanced craft tools used to measure and critique such songs as well as to plot and plan how best to "carve out" our own.

OPMC function as fine tune calibration settings for your creative GPS. Reference them early in your writing to prevent songs from stalling out. Let's breakdown each.

Opportunity

Of the four, opportunity's the most important as it's the opportunity that writing the song creates in the first place that's paramount.

The jet fuel that propels opportunity lies within the "shape of a writer's heart."

Each writer has a unique set of themes, interests, emotions, writing history, a need for self-expression, or an intellectual and historical curiosity about songs or even a sense of rivalry to beat, best, or emulate a favorite song or writer.

These strands combine and combust, turning writers into *momentum hunters* seeking those themes that "ring most true" while channeling head and heart, thinking and feeling into the raw need to harvest emotion, logic, stories, trends, and poetry.

Opportunity is the *heavy lifting tool*; it's where smart, experienced songwriters get most of their conception work done prior to getting in the trench and writing the entire song itself.

Remember:

- Good ideas get you 50% of the way to your songwriting goals.

- Great ideas get you 75% of the way to your songwriting goals.

- A brilliant idea gets you 90% of the way to your songwriting goals!

The most exciting part of songwriting *is* often the "Eureka!"—that moment of seeing a song's flight plan instantly take shape (the "how to write it" song map, from verse to prechorus, to chorus, etc.) as the idea expands in our creative consciousness.

The opportunity phase is where experience, instinct, and the practical realities of "pulling off" a song concept meet up, where it determines whether the idea contains the essential blend of the surprising and the familiar, the juice/power, uniqueness, originality and reason to qualify as a prime songwriting opportunity (i.e., how "big" the song concept can be written).

Knowing the "History" of *how* ideas have been written matters.

That knowledge leads to finding crafty ways into ideas that have been overwritten by compelling one to be inventive, or perhaps practical if deciding no, Paul McCartney owns the song title/territory of "Yesterday," so I'll pass on writing my own song titled "Yesterday."

The emotional and practical reason(s) to write the song become certified and fully answered in the nascent opportunity stage.

Good writers completely understand what the audience takeaway or response will be to a song under construction.

Again, if we take a superior, well-conceived and constructed song such as Carole King's "You've Got a Friend," as an example, we can see the song's:

Song Intention

- Is to comfort and emotionally support a friend in trouble

Core Emotion

- Reassurance

Song Category

- Reassurance/empowerment

Audience Tracking

- The Verse to Chorus/Problem-Solution Setup
- The use of "You"
- Clear visuals—the liberal use of images
- Summing Up

Use these criteria to answer questions about the foundation you're building your songs on. Typically, if you can't determine the strength of your concept, you may be building on a notion, as mentioned in chapter 2. Notions need a lot of creative surgery to turn them into valuable opportunities.

Notions are not fully realized opportunities; they're opportunities in training because:

- They don't have clear destinations.

- People can't see their lives in them.

- People don't know who to root for or why they should keep listening.

- They add thinking and kill the hypnosis process.

Learn to make the distinction of a fully "green-lit" opportunity to write that for you is "good to glow."

Your imagination and influences, your taste, and passion as a music lover cross paths with your song-writing ability and experience in this stage. Apply these frames of reference to each new song you write; your instincts will become stronger in sizing up and harvesting the core themes living in your lyrical and musical ideas.

Perspective

Van Gogh's Notebooks was a traveling exhibition hosted by the Metropolitan Museum of Art in New York City some years back. The vast amount of sketches made by the artist as a student explored depth of field, objects drawn from different distances, and points of view that revealed his understanding and the power of perspective.

What songwriters can learn and apply from understanding perspective and its myriad usages is incalculable. Perspective crosses terrain from who's singing, to when in time they are singing, to from what vantage point the singer or the audience is experiencing a song from and more.

The range and diversity perspective gives writers to add color and originality in their songs include:

1. Writing from different points of view grammatically: first, second, or third person.

2. Using time; the past, future, and present to express the evolution of emotions.

3. Writing from the "point of view" of time itself: the past, present, and future.

4. Writing from the "point of view" of physical objects: Steve Goodman's song "The City of New Orleans" or Henry Krieger's "I'm a Ball."

5. Writing from the "point of view" of values or products: Jamie O'Hara's "The Cold Hard Truth," John Mayer's "Belief," Brad Paisley's "Alcohol."

6. Writing by using objects to indicate or support a belief or need to believe in an idea, emotion, or wish: Gary Burr's "Can't Be Really Gone."

7. Changing perspectives from singing to a general audience, or third person "He" or "She" (in a verse) to "You" in a chorus as in the Script's "Breakeven" (doing so adds urgency).

8. Changing perspective from verse to verse, as in what "she" wants in a first verse to what "you" want in a second verse ("thinking out loud").

9. Using individual senses to express what is heard, seen, touched, tasted, smelled, felt, or sensed.

10. Perspective as a decision-making tool when considering how best to write song titles and ideas (see Sixteen Song Title Ideation Strategies, page 27).

11. Perspective as a "reverse melodic engineering tool": placing the end of a melodic phrase first, and the beginning of a melodic phrase last.

12. Taking the opposite point of view of a well-known song, such as "Yesterday"—instead of "I believe in yesterday," write it as "I don't believe in yesterday;" now it's a song about hope, not loss.

    This strategy should also be applied to any song that makes an impression, by asking oneself whether the opposite-side-of-the-ideas point of view has harvesting possibilities.

13. Changing one word in a famous song title, such as "As Time Goes By" to "As Tears Go By."

Perspective tools offer so many options to write personal details into your songs. We don't need to stop working the rich vein we're digging (the song concept we're writing) to go dig in another mountain (write a new idea) when the original concept is strong.

We can simple mine another perspective. This is expressed beautifully in the perspective shift in the first and second verses of "Thinking Out Loud," or in how beautifully the genesis line in "Chelsea Morning" is effectively harvested by changing one word in that line (from what she *heard*, to *saw*, to *knew*).

Take advantage of the knowledge that *songs thrive in a simple and urgent environment.* Don't throw a fist full of ideas at us, unless it's a "laundry list song" à la Bob Dylan's "Bob Dylan's 115th Dream").

Squeeze all of the toothpaste out of the tube (all the DNA of your song).

The perspective umbrella covers what's at stake for the singer singing, also the nuanced way stories can be told.

Perspective can decide the order in which details are revealed or get you out of trouble when you've written your first verse and chorus and are wondering:

- What song category your song easily falls into

- How to best start writing a second verse ("Coast" is a good example of this as it's not clear the song's a "coming-of-age" song until the second verse reveals it)

- Whether a song needs a bridge or refrain. Some songs need that defining statement, the "shout-out to an audience one last time before the song ends" that spells out the song's theme. (The bridge in the Beatles' "We Can Work It Out" is a good example.)

A song may already have enough strong hooks working their magic, making writing a bridge or refrain superfluous. Smart songwriters know which part of their songs are the strongest and use/repeat that part most.

Momentum falls into two categories: musical and lyrical.

Musical Momentum

Musical momentum is created by

- modulations

- tempo changes

- time signature changes

- cadences

- false cadences

- melodic and rhythmic variation-development tied to song form

- creating ambiguous key centers

- contemporary production and arranging techniques driving toplines/backing tracks/beats

- dynamics

- vocal harmonies

- vocal or instrumental call and response

- musical dynamics and accents

- creative approaches to mixing up song form usage

Modulation can shift up or down, creating intense musical drama. Such songs as "Breathless," performed by the Corrs, or "How Do I Live," performed by Trisha Yearwood and LeAnn Rimes, or Eric Clapton's "Layla" modulate down from chorus to verse, whereas such songs as James Horner and Will Jennings's "My Heart Will Go On," Dolly Parton's "I Will Always Love You," and Berlin's "Take My Breath Away," written by Giorgio Moroder and Tom Whitlock, use the more common upward modulation.

Songs also use larger intervals to modulate beyond a half or whole step as well, such as Desmond Child, Jon Bon Jovi, and Richard S. Sambora's "Living on a Prayer."

It's de rigueur in male/female duets to accommodate each singer's vocal range by building in modulations to make a duet plausible.

Another strong use of musical momentum is shown when switching from minor to major keys (verse: minor; chorus: major). One of the most famous and uplifting examples is the disco classic "Don't Leave Me This Way."

The sustained use over many years of repeating four-chord-based chord progressions has led to many writers creating ambiguous key centers for their songs.

An *ambiguous key center* is a chord progression that never resolves to the one, or tonic, chord of a progression. The key in which the song is in is never fully defined, only implied. This works great in songs where emotional turmoil or uncertainty drive a lyric and are mirrored by the music's uncertain "song key destination" (e.g., "Wide Awake," "Get Lucky").

For example, the chord progression in Katy Perry's "Wide Awake" (Gm11, Bb12, F, and C) would indicate that F is the song key, but the song never resolves/lands on F. Chord progressions cycling over in this fashion complement lyrics about alienation or disillusionment.

The Bacharach-David song "Promises, Promises" produces a riotous color scheme of momentum, combining a string of odd time signatures with wild intervallic modulations to create a stunning empowerment song that has stood the test of time.

A fantastic example of dynamics and accents used to create momentum is the horn arrangement of Earth, Wind & Fire's "Can't Hide Love," a classic.

Production techniques used by producers, beat makers/programmers, and arrangers also add to the arsenal of musical momentum tools employed by contemporary music makers.

Typically, this translates to the use of chords being "implied" by the strands of sound that make up the "root motion" or bass line, creating more openness in the track for vocals to breath and have greater emotional impact.

"Call and answer," the call and response between a lead singer and background vocalists, creates huge opportunities for musical momentum; consider such songs as "Wide Awake, "Shout," and "My Generation."

"Call and answer" also happens between vocalists and instruments (as a mnemonic device) in such songs as "Hallelujah I Love Her So," "Let's Go Get Stoned," and "Zat You, Santa Claus?"

The song "Get Dancing" does something quite rare in pop and dance music, its momentum comes from its chorus hook being based on three bars of 4/4. The dropping of a bar of 4/4 is original and creates surprise and freshness, as most hooks/phrases are typically based on either two or four bars of 4/4.

Single-instrument intro builds are examples of musical momentum across song form. They include:

- Starting intros with bass lines: "Don't Stop 'Til You Get Enough," "Breakeven," "Gimme Some Lovin'"

- Intros that start with guitar lines: "The Last Time," "Day Tripper," "Buckaroo"

- Intros that start with keyboard motifs: "Hot in Herre"

- Intros that start with strings: Ray Charles's "Georgia in My Mind"

A singer's performance or musical momentum can be enhanced or ensured by choosing the correct key in which a song is delivered. Singers need headroom; the ability to get 20 percent louder or softer from the medium or natural volume they deliver the body of a song at.

Lyrical Momentum

Lyrical momentum is gained by establishing and maintaining lyric relevance throughout an entire song. Balancing familiarity, surprise, poetry, and clarity keeps listeners engaged. Each word or line is either adding momentum or creating drag to the songs hypnotic potential.

Although every line in a song is important, certain lines are more so such as:

- The opening lines of a first verse (to get the listener's attention)

- The first and last line of a prechorus (to "sum up" the verse just heard, then pivot to set up the chorus)

- The downbeat line of the chorus (the "Reveal" of the song title in AABABCA song form)

- The opening lines of a second verse (adding new relevance or meaning to the song)

- The bridge or refrain (the last opportunity to "shout out" the song's underlying meaning to the listener before the song ends)

These five key spots in the song form act like the gravitational assist planets give a passing satellite: the satellite speeds up, is sling-shot forward as it's caught in the higher speed of the planet's gravitational pull. Song form performs the exact same effect on lyric lines. These key spots provide acceleration to the writer's intention.

Again, the use of "Summing Up" is a critical tool in lyrical momentum as clearly framing our meaning and intention of the lyric just written before adding a new line or concept removes any confusion. As mentioned earlier, this clarity or lyrical logic is achieved by combining two lines; one an image and one a statement or metaphor "explaining" the use of the image:

Paul Simon's "Something So Right"

- Line one: a picture—"They've got a wall in china it's a thousand miles long"

- Line two: a statement/metaphor—"To keep out the foreigners they made it strong"

Billy Seidman & Brent Anderson's "Coast"

- Line one: a picture—"That hill is now an on ramp to an interstate"

- Line two: a statement/metaphor— "Time leaves its stamp on all things in its wake"

These tools and those that define lyrical contrast help writers better understand what else needs to be said in a lyric as well as in what order to reveal a range of details and story points.

Thinking about where momentum is building in a song helps a writer make key decisions about harvesting every part of an idea. This includes knowing what needs to be included and what needs to be left out of the lyric or when it is time to introduce a new idea or point of view.

Lyrical momentum helps in determining the length of musical sections (the removal of a prechorus in a second verse, for example) or cut the fat in a lyric so writers say exactly what needs to be said and no more.

Contrast is also lyrical and musical.

Lyrical Contrast

Lyrical contrast helps maintain listener engagement and prevents audience tune-out and lyrical over-load or fatigue (from adding irrelevant information).

Leveraging lyrical contrast for maximum emotional payoff should start at the inception of songwriting, when the writer's intention and the reason the song's being written is well understood.

There are a few tools in the contrast arsenal the biggest being the use of the "problem-solution setup."

The problem-solution setup is a well-used device in many songs; one simply decides in which part of the song form to reveal the "problem" (the motive for writing the song) and in which part of the song form to reveal the "solution" (what you want to have happen in response to the problem).

- "You've Got a Friend" (problem in verse—solution in chorus)

- "Acceptance Speech" (pictures of being in love in verse—pictures of breakup in chorus)

In "breakup" songs, it may prove more powerful to start the song at the "sunnier side" when the relationship was good, so as to contrast it with the heartbreak/loss side revealed in the songs' chorus or "tag line."

Using a breakup song as an example, we have a few choices to make about where in the song we reveal the details of loss (the core emotion driving breakup songs), being:

- The coping with loss

- The anger, regret, or rejection caused by loss

- The recovery from loss, or

- The just working through "the grief in the moment" of loss

- Plus any other detail or emotion the writer needs or wants to express

One can see the advantages of this writing strategy straight off.

If we start dark, we can go darker; if we want to offend, we can get more offensive: for example, Randy Newman's "Short People."

Another way to use contrast is to describe someone's behavior/actions and then how those actions make you feel:

"You bring me breakfast in bed, plant sweet kisses on my head

And you make me feel like Christmas morning, the three, two, one on New Year's Eve"

The verse is about "him/her"; the chorus is about "you" and how those actions make you feel. The contrasting verse sets up the chorus payoff, the actions they take.

Contrast is also used to raise the energy and urgency of a chorus by writing that chorus as a list of "actions or commands," as in "Thinking Out Loud" (contrasting with the statements made in the verses and prechoruses). It is also a tool to deepen an audience's involvement in a song. First, it can be used structurally in lyric song form. Using the Beatles' "We Can Work It Out" as another example of the Problem-Solution Setup: a verse shows the problem—two lovers constantly fighting—whereas the chorus contrasts a solution—"We Can Work It Out!"

Other examples of lyrical contrast include making comparisons—comparisons between:

- Physical elements and emotions: "Our Love Is Here to Stay"

- Judgments and outcomes: "They All Laughed"

- Comparing lovers: "Why Can't He Be You"

And contrast can be used to check how and where repetition is working in a song (as in the Stones' "(I Can't Get No) Satisfaction," where the repetition of the title is spelled out in a list of times and details where "Satisfaction" is not being found.)

Musical Contrast

Contrast vitalizes storytelling. From intros to verses, prechoruses to choruses, refrains and/or bridges, the continued use of musical contrast refreshes a listener's interest by adding melodic and arranging surprises to familiar elements.

Musical arrangements, production, programing, sound selection, and mixing decisions contribute to the "familiar-surprise" setup, keeping audiences involved in a song.

As mentioned, a listener's relationship to song form is built into their DNA whether realized or not, much as water is invisible to a fish (a fish's environment being all encompassing as to be transparent or taken for granted).

Smart songwriter/producers know this and "signal" to the listener when a section of the song form is changing or about to change by adding new "sounds": instruments, frequencies, subdivided percussion or hi-hats, and chord changes to announce the chorus has arrived.

Musical contrast decisions should progress throughout the song form until the end or fadeout.

Musical contrast can be achieved in many ways, including:

- Writing punchy, staccato, or short melody notes for verses that contrast with legato, or longer-held melody notes in a chorus

- Contrasting a softly sung, low-volume verse with a roaring loudly sung and played chorus (à la Nirvana)

- Writing a bright pentatonic melody over a minor chord progression

- Writing melodies that start at the lowest part of a singer's range rising through the song form to a climax at the height of the singers range. Examples include the Righteous Brothers' "You've Lost That Loving Feeling" and Toby Keith's "We Were in Love."

- The use of rests or negative space. Example: "I Just Want to Stop."

- Stating or quoting the chorus before jumping into a song's verse, a common technique used by the Beatles in such songs as "She Loves You," "Anytime at All," and "Nowhere Man"

- Creating breakdowns to a cappella vocals

- Writing the same repeating melody notes rhythmically for an AA section (of an AABA song form, for example) contrasted with a lyrical or intervallic driven melody in the bridge or refrain, à la "One Note Samba"

- Similar to the above but using chromatic movement for the A section in AABA song form: the main title themes from the film *A Man and a Woman* and "Watch What Happens" from the film *The Umbrellas of Cherbourg* are good examples of chromatic melodic movements.

- Sometimes not creating musical contrast turns out to be a bold decision with huge "earworm" payoff! Consider the melodies of "It Had to Be You," "All of Me," or Beethoven's Fifth Symphony. All of these melodies just stick to their guns by investing in their repetition. Yes, contrast comes from the hand-off to a refrain or a new movement, but our first encounter with the prime melody is doubled down on by the composer's relentless use of it.

- The traditional verse to chorus/refrain song form: "Here, There, and Everywhere," "It Had to Be You," "Let's Call the Whole Thing Off"

Review: Opportunity, Perspective, Momentum, and Contrast

The craft tools of OPMC give songwriters fresh advantages to fully harvest, to think and rethink, concepts, and compositional approaches.

The concept of becoming a songwriting athlete in practice shows up in how perceptive a writer is to:

- The world around them

- Their knowledge of an arsenal of craft tools at their disposal

- And a long history of applying them

With practice and experimentation (writing a lot of songs), choosing the right tool for the right job from this extensive list becomes second nature.

With experience, writers quickly learn to see where opportunity, perspective, momentum, and contrast live or don't live in their songs and adjust accordingly.

The mastery of OPMC produces Emotional Hypnotism in an audience and for a writer the ability for the song to tell you exactly what it needs at all times.

The Elements of Song Craft Mastery Strategy Chart

Communication achieves emotional hypnotism.

Songs are written as a response to an event. What do you want to say about that event?

Is your intention to inspire or entertain?

SONG CATEGORIES/TYPES OF SONGS BUILD SONGS ON CORE EMOTIONS

Inspiration Songs:

- Love: New Love / Devotional / Make Up / Break Up

- Songs of Longing: Loss / Grief / Hope / Forgiveness

- Coming of Age

- Songs of Reassurance

- Empowerment Songs

- Joy: Songs of Remembrance / Romance

- Songs Based on Coming to Terms with an Event

- Songs of Regret / Revenge / Rejection / Gratitude

- Chants

- Children Songs

- Alienation / Freedom

- Anthems / Authority Songs

- Socially Conscious Songs

Event Or Holiday Songs:

- Christmas / Valentines

- Celebration Songs

Entertainment Songs:

- Party Songs

- Dance Songs

- Summer Songs

- Authority Songs

- Political Songs

- Attitude Songs: Swagger / Defiance / Confusion

Harvesting Song DNA / Song Title Ideation and Concept Development Strategies

- Genesis Line Strategy™
- Debate Team Strategy™
- Environmental Strategy™
- Single Word Song Titles
- Vignette Strategy™
- Authority Songs
- The Reveal
- Songs with Action Words in Their Titles
- Title Sandwich
- Changing One Word in a Famous Title
- Writing Your Greatest Fear
- Titles that Make Comparisons
- Intention Based or Free Association Song Strategies™
- Call—Answer Writing Strategies
- Song Form / Tag Line Strategy™
- Singing Stream of Conscious Words and Melodies
- Topline to Track
- Writing Your Greatest Joy
- Collaboration Strategies

ADVANCED SONG CRAFT STRATEGIES

Lyrical:		Melodic and Musical:

Lyrical:

- Grammar Tools™
- Editorial Tools
- Song Craft Perspective Tools
- Brief and Premise Strategies
- Creation Space vs Re-Write Space™
- Problem - Solution Tied To Song™
- Object / POV Strategies™
- From POV of Time, Values, Products
- Reverse Lyric Study™

- Musical and Lyrical Momentum
- Musical and Lyrical Contrast
- Balancing Creativity with Clarity
- Song Asset Lists
- Creative GPS™

Melodic and Musical:

- Melodic Reverse Engineering
- Melodic Profile™
- Step, Rhythmic, and Intervalic Approaches
- 3, 4, and 5 Note Motif Strategies
- Chromatic and Diminish Motion Studies
- Bass Line Driven Songs
- Intro Motif Driven
- Major to Minor Key Verse / Chorus
- Song Form Usage and Strategies

Critiquing Exercise #7 "Acceptance Speech"

Critique the song "Acceptance Speech," using the craft tools of OPMC as well as those introduced in previous chapters. After your critique is made, compare it to the one-sheet questionnaire following the song lyric.

"Acceptance Speech" ▶

Sarah Bonsignore: music; Billy Seidman: lyric and music

> Holding hands as we ran toward the ocean
> Watching waves break in slow-motion
> Just one scene from our endless bliss
> Before all the signs I missed
> I've got so much to say but I'll keep it brief
>
> (CHORUS)
> It's time for my acceptance speech
> Some stars are just out of reach
> Some hearts you never get to keep
> And some dreams you've got to let go of
>
> No matter how hard I tried
> How I needed you by my side
> I know we can never be
> That's my acceptance speech
> My acceptance speech
>
> Searched your face for my place in our future
> All I saw was you turn away from me
> Gave you space to figure us out
> Living with hope then endless doubt
> Now I'm past that stage and I turn the page
> To give

(CHORUS)

Raise sails on a ship that sank

Got friends, family, and god to thank

For helping to make me see

My future's now up to me

That's my acceptance speech

My acceptance speech

Copyright © 2017 Pleasurecraft MP (BMI)/Fearless Rose Publishing (BMI)

"Acceptance Speech" Questionnaire

Use the Song Craft tools of:

- OPMC

- Creative GPS

- SAA Critiquing Tool #1

To answer the following questions about the songs lyrical and musical construction, and how the songs concept, title, and DNA were harvested.

1. Related to opportunity, how was the song title reimagined and used differently than its general everyday use or understanding?

2. How many words and pictures related to the term 'Acceptance Speech" do you see used in the song lyric?

3. Where in the song form (verses, pre-chorus, chorus, refrain/coda) do these related words and pictures associated with an actual acceptance speech show up?

4. How is the Problem-Solution Setup used in the lyric construction of the song?

5. Related to perspective, where in the song form does the singer sing either directly to the subject (the person the song is being sung to) or to a general audience?

6. Related to lyrical contrast, what song category does the song start out as?

7. What song category does the song end up in?

8. How does the song's melody develop tied to the song form? Where in the song form, (verses, pre-chorus, chorus, refrain/coda) do you notice the use or development of step, rhythmic, and intervallic melodic motion?

9. What's the vocal range of the song?

10. What does the singer want to happen by singing the song? (Intention)

11. What "Core Emotion" seems to be driving the song?

Study the song and write down your answers. Compare them to the answers on page 90.

Writing Prompt #3

Spend time reviewing different ideas that are important for you to write about and that you know an audience wants to hear. Translate that importance, urgency, or interest in your idea into a song title. Then, write that song.

Know the opportunity in writing your song.

Then, use the song craft mechanics of perspective, momentum, and contrast to connect it together!

What emotion do you want people hearing the song to feel?

What's the song in service of? Feeling acceptance? hope? regret? etc.

Let's just enjoy the moment!

What kind of song is it? A party song? a falling-in-love song? a breakup song? a makeup song? a coming-of-age song? a "love me in spite of my issues" song? etc.

Are you using original images, painting word pictures, and writing words that sound the way people actually talk to each other?

Why do you need to write it? What real experience is it reflecting in your life? Look to come up with a song title that offers an "Opportunity" to writing it in a surprising way.

Use song form to "speed up" your storytelling. If you're writing in a pop format, you're writing: hook 1 (verse), hook 2 (chorus 1 [big]), hook 3 (chorus 2 [bigger!]).

Answers to the "Acceptance Speech" Questionnaire

1. Related to opportunity, how was the song title reimagined and used differently than its general everyday use or understanding?

    A: *It's a surprising twist to use a concept associated with a thank you (as acceptance speeches are) as a concept used to come to terms with personal loss.*

    The big "opportunity" here is the surprise that makes it a strong idea without having to explain, merely show the loss with well-placed pictures/images and statements.

2. How many words and pictures related to the term "Acceptance Speech" do you see used in the song lyric?

    A: *Three.*

3. Where in the song form (verses, pre-chorus, chorus, refrain/coda) do these related words and pictures associated with an actual acceptance speech show up?

    A: *In the first pre-chorus or "tag" to the verse: "I've got so much to say but I'll keep it brief."*

    In the second pre-chorus or "tag" to the 2nd verse: "Now I'm past that stage and I turn the page to give."

    In the refrain/coda: "Got friends, family, and God to thank for helping"

4. How is the Problem-Solution Setup used in the lyric construction of the song?

    A: *In reverse, the chorus is dark and shows the "The Problem," so the verse to create "contrast" is light—"The Solution."*

5. Related to perspective, where in the song form does the singer sing either directly to the subject (the person the song is being sung to) or to a general audience?

    A: *The verses are typically sung here to the subject, and the chorus and refrain/coda are sung to the general audience.*

6. Related to lyrical contrast, what song category does the song start out as?

   A: *Breakup Song.*

7. What song category does the song end up in?

   A: *Empowerment Song.*

8. How does the song's melody develop tied to the song form? Where in the song form, (verses, pre-chorus, chorus, refrain/coda) do you notice the use or development of step, rhythmic, and intervallic melodic motion?

   A: *In the verses, it uses a step-driven melody within a pentatonic scale. In the chorus, it moves higher in the register, adding a more intervallic-driven and rhythmic-driven approach.*

9. What's the vocal range of the song?

   A: *An octave and a second.*

10. What does the singer want to happen by singing the song? (Intention)

    A: *Come face to face with the loss of a deep love, accept it, and begin to build a new future based on thier will to overcome the loss.*

11. What "Core Emotion" seems to be driving the song?

    A: *Loss, acceptance, survival.*

General Notes about Acceptance Speech

Writing about "The One that Got Away" is a powerful decision/Opportunity. Why?

Because everyone, no matter thier social status, good looks, privilege or lack of it, has loved someone deeply who could not love them back in the way they needed to be loved.

The hurt of that loss and your ability to write your own experience of loss in pictures, in service of honestly trying to sort out "coming to terms with it" or making a clear decision about your response to it, is a powerful lure to a mass audience.

6

Four Chords and the Loop

Production, Sound, Programming, Arranging, and Collaboration in Contemporary Pop Songwriting

The sound itself, the production, is of such great importance that it has become an integrated part of the composition. —Max Martin

The blur of roles played in the creation of contemporary songs continues a trend started in the early 1960s, when artists on a mass scale starting writing their own.

Technology's played a huge hand in accelerating how songs and records are made today, with individual collaborators wearing multiple hats while contributing musical, lyrical, vocal, musician, programming, engineering, and production roles in contemporary songwriting.

Prior to the 1960s, traditional records played on radio and released to the public had many people performing specific roles: the composer, lyricist, recording artist, record producer, arranger, A&R director, copyist, musician contractor, vocal contractor, musicians, singers, recording engineer, mixing engineer, and mastering engineer.

Many records are still made this way, though the predominance of music songwriters make and the public currently hears is based on radical changes brought by the evolution of technology and music software development. This has revolutionized not only how writers collaborate but the musical trends, styles, sounds, and vocabulary that define what it means to be a songwriter, producer, composer, lyricist, and musician today.

Here's a breakdown of roles today's songwriters take when competing to place songs on radio, playlists, sync licenses, and other commercial formats.

Much of the following is based on excerpts from conversations with Jon Buscema, a Los Angeles–based producer-songwriter-musician and former student.

Jon's exceptional abilities as a producer, songwriter, musician, and mixer become evident to anyone who works with him. His work ethic, attention to detail, and collaboration skills make him a highly sought-after collaborator in the LA and New York music market.

Process: Track and Beat Makers

Track and beat makers collectively can be considered the "studio musicians" of today, delivering sounds and beats for a variety of projects.

Such records as "Lucid Dreams" by Juice WRLD is an example of beats and tracks/sounds made seamless on a current pop record.

From genre to genre, beat makers can play different roles. In hip-hop, beat makers can make beats that other people write over, but may never be in the same room with people using them. Beat makers are basically delivering everything but melody and lyrics.

Pop music has become more hip-hop oriented in that it is becoming more "loop" based.

Loop-based production encourages chord simplification, though perhaps that tread can or will in time swing back to include more complex progressions.

The huge influence of technology can be seen through the brevity of songs and even on the song form itself, with the loss of bridges in contemporary songs and the information usually contained in bridges. All a direct result of people making music in a computer and it being made easier and more accessible to do.

The Developing Producer/Programmer/ Songwriter/Musician/Vocalist

Successful contemporary pop musicians typically take one of two paths: going on the road or (in New York) playing Broadway shows, or becoming producers and programmers, where their musicianship (guitar playing, bass, keyboard skills, vocal, or other) serves their production and songwriting collaborations.

Recording sessions that sustained and gave employment to hundreds upon hundreds of musicians and singers for many generations, now employ only a select group.

In the past forty years, the education of musicians, singers, songwriters, producers, and engineers in popular music at the college level has led to alumni networks that support employment opportunities for select talented former students.

The career advancement path for producers starts with lots of listening by yourself.

Listening by picking apart everything you hear on records you love—the instruments, chords, lyrics, vocals, processing, parts, sounds, mixes—but, just as important, figuring out "Why" those choices are there and how they function. Why are certain sounds prevalent at certain times to add energy, drama, tension, or release" There's always a reason for them being there, so learn what that reason is.

Production also take its cues from a song's music and lyrics, so be on the lookout for ways to enhance what's built into the song itself.

Learn to finish your productions, because if you always stop at doing 80 percent, you'll never practice how to bring the final 20 percent to completion. Technology is also a huge and ever-changing tool in a producer's hands.

Role of Traditional Music Producer in Contemporary Music

Traditional producers can play a variety of roles. They can be executive producers, "vision keepers" functioning as project managers, who hold various groups of collaborators on message with a project's overall concept or evolving concept (e.g., Max Martin, Ricky Reed).

They can also jump in and wear one of many hats: lyricist, composer, programmer, engineer, mixer, or musician, depending on what a song needs or his or her particular strength.

In the most traditional music industry sense, the producer is responsible for delivering hits to the record label who hires him or her, signed the artist, and funds the project.

The Tools of Sound

Sonics have evolved. Songs have become more spacious to accommodate how production and technology have changed. The availability of cloud-based sample libraries, such as Splice and Arcade, has made access to sounds used on hit records easier to acquire. With additional samples being added constantly to subscription-based libraries from users everywhere, famous producers use them in their production as well in some cases, make their samples available.

This compares to the past thirty years, when curated sound libraries were the private domain of producers and engineers. That said, of course many current producers, engineers, and mixers curate and collect sounds.

A case can be also made that sounds used on records need to sound more interesting than good. Also, the making of samples doesn't need to be based on great musicianship but on programing and processing tricks that create an interesting musical part. The bottom line with sound is to come up with whatever you want as long as the end result is creative, interesting, unique, and different.

Contemporary Collaborations

Typically, collaborations happen with three to five people in a room and everyone has a different job to do. The job you take on can and will change from session to session, even if your primary role is producer/programmer, topliner, vocalist, lyricist, or musician. This is because, some days, you'll be working with other producer/programmers, topliners, vocalists, lyricists, or musicians. When that happens, your role is to find your best role for that session.

Good sessions come from the ease in which ideas flow and everyone contributes to the making of a song, so that by the end, typically three or four hours, everyone's stoked about the song.

If you're writing with artists, you'll know what their sound is and they'll have an idea of what they want to make that day. Each collaborator listens to a few of the artists' songs, making mental notes or talking about what kind of songs might add to enhance the range of songs the artists need for their project.

If writing to come up with a song to pitch, it's best to just start talking about what's going on in everyone's life and hear what anyone in the room is feeling strongly about and write that.

In this instance, producer/programmers can take their cue from the emotion generated by that idea to choose sounds, tempo, and mood to start building a track with.

Often it's a producer making a beat, while a topliner freestyles to it or a producer comes in with a track finished or mostly finished, and everyone toplines to that. Lots of times, artists just freestyle for hours and the producer comps, makes a compilation, the best parts. At some point, craft or editorial come into play to mold the song.

This can be challenging but for example, if you're a topliner or lyricist and someone comes up with a lyric you dislike, your first instinct might be to say that, but the vibe in the room needs to develop, so saying nothing is the smart act. There will be time to circle back and address this in a respectful way and often, there is no need to, as the song could go in a completely different writing direction. The rhythm of coming up with a group consensus of what kind of song is getting written between three to five people can be challenging.

Finishing Songs in Sessions with Three to Five Collaborators

The producer/track/beat maker has a lot of control in deciding what in the end of the session equals a song worth the effort to keep working on. Generally, if everybody on the session is excited by a song, that consensus is enough for a producer to keep working on the track; if not, the producer puts his or her energy into other songs from other sessions.

Making a Living as a Track/Beat Maker

It's very difficult to make a living as a pure songwriter unless you have hit songs. You can have success with big cuts (cuts by famous artists but not on radio), and even with a publisher representing you, after a few years, if your work does not translate into hit radio cuts regardless of talent, it's common to be cut loose by a publisher. This leads to songwriters with a level of success having to keep a day job.

Producers/track/beat makers, on the other hand, have a monetizable skill set. They can mix songs, or produce songs for artists or other songwriters and record labels. Talented P/T/B (producer/track/beat makers) whose careers are developing measure the value-to-cost to benefit project by project. Another area that keeps both songwriters and P/T/B in the green is syncs. Sync licensing is the transaction made between songwriters, music publishers, and owners of master recordings for songs and tracks to be used in film, TV, and commercials. This income keep lots of developing midlevel or successful writers in music. Sync fees can range from a few thousand dollars to tens of thousands for well-known, popular songs. Tracks for syncs can be songs or nonvocal instrumentals. Teaching is another side hustle for all good songwriters, P/T/B keeping them in the game. Some of the best career opportunities come from working with extremely talented people without resources to pay what a strong midlevel P/T/B services are worth, but here is where the value-to-cost ratio is important to get right; you never know where a gig will lead, who you'll meet, where a project can go, so keeping an open mind to collaborations and compensation is good business.

Types of Copyright Ownership Splits in Contemporary Compositions

Common practice in writing sessions is everyone in the room gets an equal share of ownership in the song created during a session.

Negotiating can arise from many scenarios, such as if a song is started by one set of writers and one writer cannot participate in the next session to finish the song, or a new writer comes in or is added to the song; or the song is liked by a label, artist, manager, and so on, who wants changes and additions made or the song to be added to the workload of another set of producers.

Some people take the traditional approach that a song copyright is based on melody and lyric; others recognize the role of production, track, and beat making (sound) as a major contributor to a song's success in this market. The truth is, there are no absolute rules on copyright ownership in the current Wild West environment where many people come into the song-making process at all levels of its creative development from demos to masters to release.

A good rule of thumb is to remain civil. Chances are, during the course of a career you will be working with many of the same people you start a song with, and keeping good working relationships matters in a community as small as the music business.

By nature, P/T/B spend more time working on a song after a session and as a result, if the song becomes used in a project, a song release of a sync license, then P/T/B are entitled to a production fee. Production fees are always subject to negotiation, however; regarding syncs, a production fee is half of the total money received for the use of a song: half being for the right typically considered to sync the composition of the song itself, the copyright; the other half, for the "master use" fee to sync the actual recording of the song. If one received $10,000 for a sync fee, half would be shared by all the songwriters on the song, the other half kept by the P/T/B who programmed the track. Now, there can be costs or percentages needed to be paid off the top for the creation of the master recording as well if that track used, outside singers or musicians, or copyrighted samples owned by other companies. In lieu of a good team—a manager, a publisher, an attorney, people who will fight and look after your interests—it does pay to take a few precautions to protect your interests: record voice memos of sessions, have a paper trail of lyrics and a listing of collaborators on songs, keep good notes or calendar notes of schedules of sessions. Once a song becomes valued in a project, lots of twists and turns can develop. No need for paranoia, but also, making smart choices to protect one's interest in song ownership is good practice.

7
Melodic Studies

Melody is a form of remembrance. It must have a quality of inevitability in our ears.
—Gian Carlo Menotti

Music is when a beautiful woman walks into a room and everyone turns their head to stare at her.
Lyrics are when the beautiful woman opens her mouth and has something to say.
—from the film *Music and Lyrics*

The tools presented in this chapter make distinctions about how to listen to and write memorable melodies. Readers are encouraged to experiment with these approaches to gain expertise and a deeper understanding of melodic construction.

Use these perspectives to critique and study the melodies of your favorite tunesmiths. Doing so, with practice will lead to enhancing and improving your natural melodic abilities.

Like a good lyric, strong melodies proffer a signature combination of the surprising and the familiar; just as lyricists return over again to familiar emotions and themes, so too are composers drawn to patterns in their melody writing.

The pathway back to the roots of how or why composers come to write a melody are typically tied to the history of the songs and compositions they've come to love that resonate with them from childhood to adulthood, that and formal training and personal study over time.

The attachment each generation has to its own unique rhythmic heritage is a factor in melody creation (much as whatever country one was born in, one learns the native language and simultaneously, the country's culture and values).

Composers typically fall into one of three melody-writing categories:

- Step

- Rhythmic

- Intervallic

Knowing what type of melody writing comes most naturally helps to frame what ingredient(s) are present in one's melodies and what elements can be added to craft that "form of remembrance and quality of inevitability." Great melodies need to incorporate all three to become transcendent. The definitions for step-, rhythmic-, and intervallic-based melodic approaches are:

Step-Driven Melodies

Step-based melody writers gravitate toward using *ascending and descending stepwise motion* of closely related notes in a scale (contour). The following songs are examples of step-driven melodies:

- "Where Is Love?" (from the musical *Oliver!*)

- "Morning Has Broken"

- "God Bless America"

- The classic '60s song "A Groovy Kind of Love" (based heavily on the Rondo movement of Sonatina in G Major, op. 36, no. 5, by Muzio Clementi)

- Gabriel Fauré's "Pavane"

- "Fields of Gold"

- "Three Blind Mice"

- "Killing Me Softly" (the A section)

Examples of Step-Driven Melodies

Step melodies tend to typically stay within an octave range, making them easy to sing.

Step melodies are defined by close, single-note scale degree movement, as you can see by these examples, as opposed to melodies built on repeating two-note motifs, such as "Nowhere Man" or "Riders on the Storm."

There seems to be a simple and familiar logic to step melodies. Study the melodies of Irving Berlin (a giant in the American songwriting pantheon), and the scale seems to produce for him a magical harvest of memorability. One underlying factor in this magic is the root motion (the bass lines) supporting the melodic movement, which we'll look at closer later in this chapter.

Of course, songs that start out utilizing a step approach need, for the sake of variation and novelty (*novella*, Italian for "piece of news" / "new idea"), to add rhythmic and intervallic movement as a song progresses.

Rhythmic-Driven Melodies

Rhythmic-based melody writing speaks for itself: "Fascinating Rhythm," "I Got Rhythm," "Rhythm of the Night," "Rhythm of My Heart." Like the fossil record in the Burgess Shale, each generation adds its own layer or variation to rhythm—hearing it, feeling it, cannibalizing it—slightly differently from the generation before. Add time to that equation; even a hundred years, and rhythm and syncopation sound radically different.

The flappers of the 1920s danced to rhythms that sound like cartoon music by today's standards of rhythm. At the time, they were the freshest, most sophisticated syncopations the world had ever produced.

Wind the rhythm clock almost a hundred years later and compare Taylor Swift's 2015 "Bad Blood" or SZA's "The Weekend" to the Original Dixieland Jazz Band's "Dixie Jass Band One Step." The point is, feel changes.

Originality is rare; most everything we hear is vocabulary rearranged (slang), not necessarily new words. (What's always original, though, is each new generation's young audience with no history to tell the profound from the cliché till experience informs or catches up to their tastes.)

Rhythm and syncopation seem to represent the roots of each generation's musical originality. That said, the retro use of sounds, baselines, tempos, samples, and rhythms of generations once or twice removed are often "rediscovered" and freshen an artist's creativity and/or "competitive advantage."

Prime examples: Bruno Mars's "Uptown Funk" and "24 Carat Magic" pay homage to the '80s sounds of the System; and Billy Joel's "The Longest Time," to '50s doo-wop vocal groups.

Examples of Rhythmic-Driven Melodies

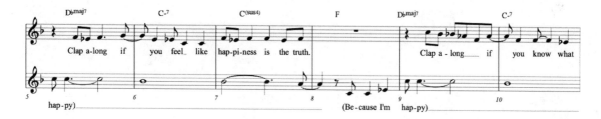

"Better Now" ›

♩ = 145 **Pop**

Music & Lyrics by
Billy Walsh, Louis Bell, Adam King Feeney and Austin Post

You prob - 'ly think that you are

CHORUS
Cm
bet - ter now,___ bet - ter now,___ you on - ly say that 'cause I'm

F
not a - round,___ not a - round,___ you know I ne - ver meant to

B♭
let you down,___ let you down,___ would-a gave you a - ny - thing,

E♭
would-a gave you ev - 'ry - thing you know I say that you are

Cm
bet - ter now,___ bet - ter now,___ I on - ly say that 'cause you're

F
not a - round,___ not a - round,___ You know I ne - ver meant to

B♭
let you down,___ let you down,___ would-a gave you a - ny - thing,

E♭
would-a gave you ev - 'ry - thing, oh whoa_____

In reality, rhythm is to music what air is to birds: so pervasive as to be taken for granted.

But as songwriting athletes and students of song, our job is to be present to see and use rhythmic opportunity—in this case, ways to harvest melodic rhythm.

Critique, study, or emulate the following songs, play them on your instrument of choice to break them down, and play with their components—the results will be revealing and inspiring.

Intervallic-Driven Melodies

Dramatic interval leaps are prime performance territory for singers with large vocal ranges and define intervallic-based melody writing. The intervallic approach is dramatic and makes for some of the most memorable songs in the historic vocal repertoire including:

- "Alfie"

- "Somewhere over the Rainbow"

- "Thinking Out Loud"

- "I Will Always Love You"

- "I'll Never Love This Way Again"

- "Somewhere"

- "The Star-Spangled Banner"

- "How Do I Live"

- "My Heart Will Go On"

All are stellar examples of intervallic-driven melody writing.

Examples of Intervallic-Driven Melodies

"Alfie" ▶

"How Do I Live" ▶

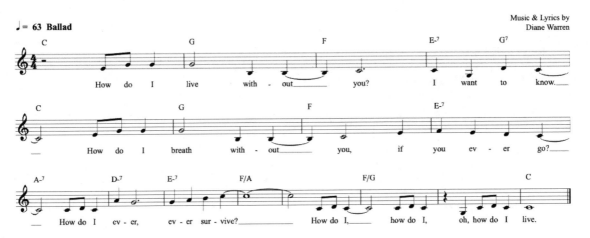

Any note's relationship to another note represents an interval, of course; that said, composing large leaps between notes or interesting chromatic (half-step or diminish) movement is a technique that also make for standout melodies.

The use of half-step intervals as passing tones (approach notes) to prime chord notes wherever they fall in the scale, adds surprise and uniqueness and is featured prominently in universally loved melodies, including:

- "White Christmas" (the opening melody)

- "If This Isn't Love" (from the musical *Finian's Rainbow*; the turnaround cadence)

- "It Had to Be You," a strong example of chromatic (half-step) melodic movement

Listening to a melody, framing it with a step, rhythmic, or intervallic overlay reveals that many well-known melodies—"earworms"—start with a step approach, then hand off to the rhythmic, and finish with intervallic. Many famous melodies also marry the step and rhythmic from the downbeat of the first chorus notes.

Music psychologist Kelly Jakubowski identifies three main reasons that melodies stand out: it comes down to pace—up-tempo rhythm (rhythmic); the shape of the melody (often called contour, what is referred to here as step); and a few unique intervals that either repeat or have large register movement (intervallic).

A jarring or surprising set of intervals surrounded by calmer, lyrical waters infused with rhythm pulls all three approaches together in such songs as "Maria," "Greensleeves," "The Entertainer," and many others. Contemplate and critique these melodies and song structures, make a list of your own for study purposes, and apply in your next composition.

Incorporating All Three Melodic Approaches: Step, Rhythmic, and Intervallic

The following melody incorporates all three—step-wise motion, rhythmic motion, and intervallic-driven melodies—seamlessly.

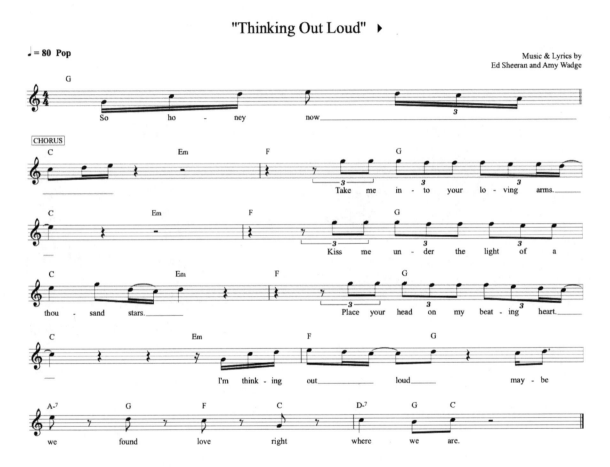

"Thinking Out Loud"

Music & Lyrics by
Ed Sheeran and Amy Wadge

Building Melodies on Motifs Starting from Different Beats of a Chorus

Songs and techniques to study include

- The use of rhythmic *repetitive single notes* at the start of a chorus melody:

Examples: "Teenage Dream," "Crazy in Love," "The Letter," "If You Don't Know Me by Now," "(Your Love Keeps Lifting Me) Higher and Higher," "Blank Space," "Sitting on the Dock of the Bay," "Bad Blood," "The Trolley Song," "You're the One That I want," "Long Before I Knew You" (from the musical *Bells Are Ringing*); the title theme to *A Man and a Woman*.

- The use of rhythmic repetitive single notes in the middle of a chorus melodic phrase:

Examples: Pharrell Williams's "Happy," Michael Jackson's "Don't Stop 'Til You Get Enough," the Brothers Osborne's "It Ain't My Fault"

- Use of rhythmic repetitive single notes at the end of a chorus melody:

Examples: the Kinks' "You Really Got Me," Katy Perry's "Wide Awake"

- Starting a chorus melody on pickup notes (from the bar before the start of the melodic phrase). Examples: the Police's "Every Little Thing She Does Is Magic," "You Can't Hurry Love"

Building Melodies on Five-, Four-, and Three-Note Motifs

- Examples of melodies built using five-note rhythmic motifs: "Every Breath You Take," "It Had to Be You," "Strangers in the Night," "I'll Be Seeing You," "That'll Be the Day," "It's Now or Never," "Please Mister Postman" (5 repetitive notes), "I Love Rock 'n' Roll," "A Broken Wing," "Breathe"

- Examples of melodies built using four-note rhythmic motifs: "Can't Buy Me Love," "Mr. Sandman" "Autumn Leaves," the Rolling Stones' "(I Can't Get No) Satisfaction," "I'm Your Venus," "There's Your Trouble"

- Examples of melodies built using three-note rhythmic motifs: The Beatles' "She Loves You," "Let It Snow," "All of Me," "Baby Love," "Yesterday" "All Night Long," "Missing You," "I Like It, I Love It"

- Songs using quarter note triplet Rhythm (To heighten emotion or to add variation): "Missing You," "Thinking Out Loud" (chorus), "We Can Work It Out" (end of bridge-refrain)

"All Of Me" ▶

Rests: Negative Space

Add to this mix the lack of melody—the negative spaces rests create in music, which are easily overlooked.

What's withheld from the ear is just as valuable as what it hears.

Rests, in their own way, are as invisible as water is to a fish; they seem to write themselves into our melodies once the notes and rhythms we need are in place.

What we don't hear sets up our experience of what we do. Become more aware of rests; they are elements of rhythmic and melodic stealth. Here are a few songs that use them in effective, subversive ways; also as pneumatic devices.

- "I Just Want to Stop"

- "Cold Sweat"

- "One Love"

- "Stop in the Name of Love"

- "Stop, Look, Listen to Your Heart"

Examples of Songs Using Rests and Negative Space in Their Melodies

"One Love" ▶

Music & Lyrics by
Bob Marley

Call and Response

Another tool in the melodic arsenal worth keeping close at hand is the use of call and response. Call and response shows up in familiar and surprising places.

Familiar: in choruses:

- "Gimme Some Lovin'" performed by the Spencer Davis Group

- "Happy" performed by Pharrell Williams

- "Respect" performed by Aretha Franklin

- "Rolling in the Deep" performed by Adele

- "My Sweet Lord" performed by George Harrison

- "Why Not Me" performed by Wynonna

- "The Shape of You" performed by Ed Sheeran

- "Son of a Preacher Man" performed by Dusty Springfield

- "I Say a Little Prayer for You" performed by Dionne Warwick

- "Help" performed by the Beatles

- "Wide Awake" performed by Katy Perry

Examples of Songs Utilizing Call and Response

"Gimme Some Lovin'" ▶

Also surprising when used as an instrument or an instrumental arrangement answer to a vocal chorus:

- "Natural Woman," performed by Carole King (string arrangement)

- "Cold Sweat" performed by James Brown (horn section arrangement)

- "My Sharona" (chorus responds to bass/guitar lick call), performed by the Knack

Root Motion: A Bass Note's Relationship to Each Melody Note

Listening to John Lennon's "Lucy in the Sky with Diamonds" and Miles Davis's Gil Evans arrangement of "Quiet Nights" reveals a startling discovery about melody: it's the *root motion, the movement of the bass notes* that primarily defines a melody, not necessarily the chords. There is no suggestion here that chords, harmony, or counterpoint are unimportant, they are in many ways, including rhythmic accompaniment, adding color/support, or in the use of arpeggiating accompaniment, for example. (And I'm sure I left a few others out.)

Using the "root" or bass note to define a melody, not the 3rd, 4th, 5th, 6th, flatted 7, natural 7th, or the "upper partials" (natural, flatted, or sharped: 9th, 11th, 13th) is a melodic writing technique to take good advantage of.

It's been liberally used as a chromatic descending tool in countless songs: "Michelle," "Stairway to Heaven," the theme to *A Man and a Woman* ("Watch What Happens"), Cole Porter's "It's All Right with Me."

Of course, the intervals of the melody may be part of the chords or chord progression, but the basic shape of a melody is defined by the movement of the bass line supporting each note. Let's look at a few examples:

"Maria" ▶

Music by Leonard Bernstein
Lyrics by Stephen Sondheim

"One Note Samba"

♩ = 144 **Samba**

Music & Lyrics by
A. Jobim

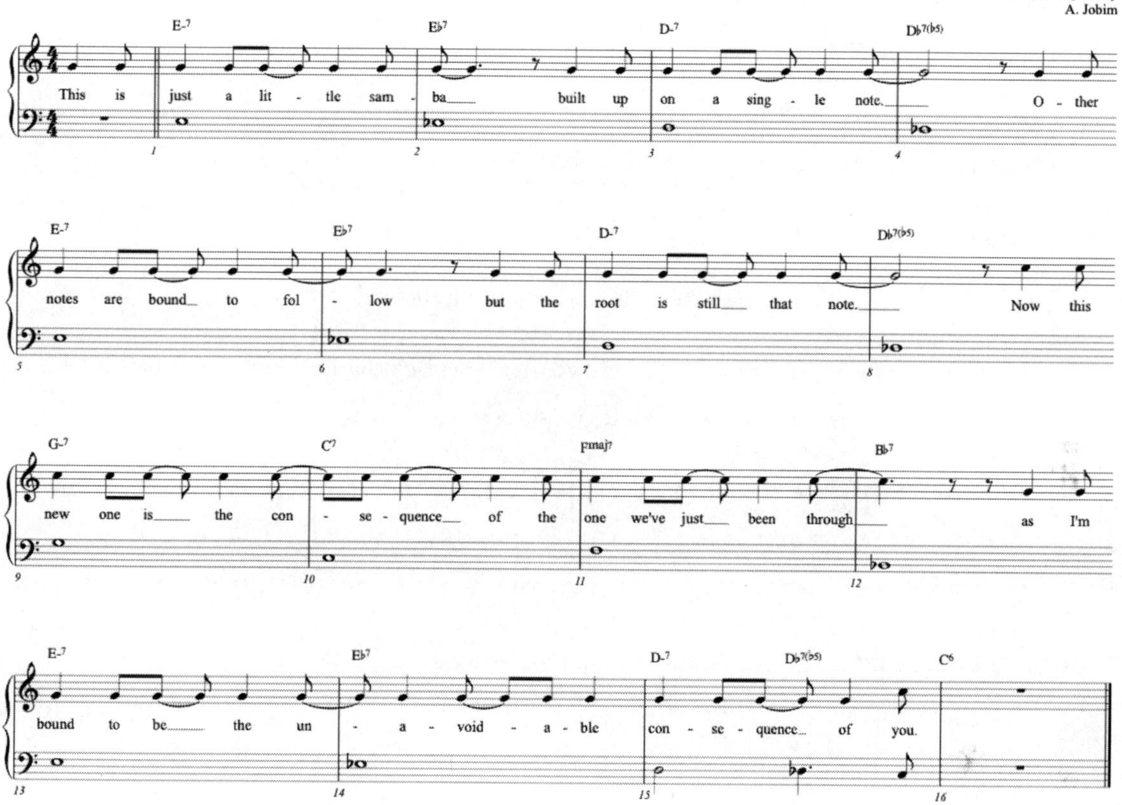

Technique for Nonmusicians to Find Chord Progressions for Songs

This approach is a practical way for songwriters who are not strong musicians (e.g., can't play chords on piano or guitar at tempo) to discover the root chords to their melodies. It's also a fine technique to go "off-roading," or improvising to write unique melodies.

If you fall into this category, try this:

- Sit at a keyboard or piano and slowly start singing the melody to a song you're writing.

- While doing so, hunt and peck on the lower keys of the keyboard for a bass note that sounds right to your ear as the note that *supports* your melody.

- Do this for each section of your song until you've found a bass note supporting the melody in each part of your song (the verse, prechorus, chorus, etc.). This will give you your song's chord progression. Make a recording of that.

Since many people hear a different set of chord progressions under a melody, doing this will act as a guide, showing a collaborator or musician how you hear your song's chord progression. This approach takes the guesswork out of finding the right chords for your songs.

Phrasing: Chorus Melodies Starting on Different Beats within a Two-Bar Phrase

Starting melodies on different beats of a bar offers great opportunities to create strong melodies.

For our purposes, let's count a bar of 4/4 as eighth notes like this:

1 + 2 + 3 + 4 + (1, 2, 3, 4 representing the downbeats and + the "up" beats). 1 *and* 2 *and* 3 *and* 4.

And 6/8 as: 1 2 3 4 5 6

- A review of Bacharach and David's "Anyone Who Had a Heart," a song in 5/4, starts the melody on beat **2**.

- Bacharach and David's "I Say a Little Prayer for You" in 4/4 reveals the melody starting on beat **2**.

- "How Do I Live": the melody starts on beat **2**.

- For Bob Marley's "One Love," the chorus melody starts on **2**, a full quarter note prior to the first note of sung melody.

- "The Shape of You": the melody in 4/4 starts on the *and* of **2** or (**2 and**).

- "Call Me Maybe," again in 4/4: the melody chorus starts on beat **2**. (See a pattern here?)

- "You're So Vain": the melody starts on beat **3**.

- "Hurts So Good": the melody starts on beat **3**.

- "Embraceable You": the melody, in 4/4, starts on the *and* of **1** or (**1 and**).

- "And I Love Her": You can make a case for the chorus melody in 4/4 starting on beat **4** without calling it a pickup. Very rare for a chorus melody to start so late in a bar.

Utilizing Whole Notes

Writing melodies with long, extended single melody notes sustaining over three beats or longer show up as passion in the ears of audience and should be used in melodies where appropriate. This can turn a two-bar phrase into a four-bar phrase as well.

Don't underestimate this power; again, it reads and sounds like commitment and urgency to a listener. Smart writers are not afraid to "hug a whole note!" Examples include:

- The Beatles' "I Should Have Known Better"

- Vince Gill's "Go Rest High on That Mountain"

- "Without You," written by Pete Ham and Tom Evans, performed by Badfinger and Harry Nilsson

Example of Melody Utilizing Whole Notes

"Without You" ▶

Chromatic Melodic Movement

Writers looking to create melodies that stand out and last could look closely at using chromatic motion in their songs. *Chromatic motion* refers to the use of semitone, or half-step intervals. This can be for a range of notes, say, from C, D-flat, D, E-flat, E, or through an entire twelve-note scale. Examples of chromatic melody movement are:

- "Habanera" from Georges Bizet's *Carmen*

- "Entry of the Gladiators" by Julius Fučík

- "Flight of the Bumblebee" by Nikolai Rimsky-Korsakov

- "Caravan" by Duke Ellington

These compositions use chromatic movement in conjunction with step, rhythmic, and intervallic movement to produce a range of memorable hook-laden melodies.

Some of Cole Porter's most famous songs, such as "Let's Do It," "Night and Day," and "So in Love," use chromatic melodic approaches; some, combined with diminished chords, add a rich haunting appeal to his songs. (The refrain of "You Do Something to Me," or the descending tag melody of "So in Love," come to mind.)

Melodies that combine chromatic and intervallic movement to great effect are "This Nearly Was Mine" and "Some Enchanted Evening" from the musical *South Pacific*, "The Pink Panther Theme," and "The James Bond Theme."

Melodic Development: Phrasing Tied to Song Form

Just as Summing Up" is tied to song form in lyric writing (so audiences understand ones meaning before adding a new meaning), so too is the development of melodic phrasing tied to song form.

If we take the song "Thinking Out Loud" and follow its melodic development over its entire length (song form), a few features become obvious. The song has five distinct melodic hooks:

1. The verse melody

2. Prechorus one melody

3. Prechorus two melody

4. Chorus melody

5. Chorus "tag" melody

This meets the general criteria of delivering four to six memorable melodic "hooks" in a contemporary pop song.

Note the factors making the melody memorable:

- The melodic phrasing of each part is repetitive.

- The melody continues to rises higher in the register as the song moves from verse to prechorus to chorus to chorus tag.

- The verse melody is based on step-driven melodic motion.

- The first prechorus melody adds more rhythmic and intervallic motion for contrast.

- The second prechorus returns to primarily step-wise motion while maintaining the melody in a now established higher register.

- The chorus delivers the highest notes in the song along with a triplet feel for added urgency and emotional expression. Good combination of quarter note step and rhythmic motion.

Learn to listen for melodic development tied to song form; the results will be revealing.

Momentum, contrast, and repetition are all huge contributing factors in creating hook-driven memorable melodies.

While composing, keep an eye on how you're spreading out the use of step, rhythmic, and intervallic movement in your melodies throughout your song (the song form).

For example, if you're a fan of classic Brazilian music, look how "One Note Samba" utilizes repetition and root motion movement to great effect; how its simplicity is contrasted by a more complex bridge melody to give the song added momentum. The same can be said of Billy Preston's "You Are So Beautiful to Me," and many other songs.

Melodic Reverse-Engineering Techniques

This is a strategy for generating melodic ideas based on preexisting song melodies. Here's how it works. Select a song you like that is in the public domain. Play or sing the main melody of the selected song, then sing the back part of the phrase first and the first part of the melodic phrase last. Play the reversed phrase on an instrument until the new melody feels and sounds workable.

Experiment by adding different chords to the reversed melody you've selected than the original chords.

This leads to more experimentation. New melodies having little in common with the original reversed melody that was engineered develop as well as surprising chord progressions.

A Note to Composers/Songwriters Who Are Not Singers

Oftentimes, composers and songwriters who don't consider themselves singers don't write melodies with large interval leaps because they themselves cannot perform them. As a composer, let the song write the melody, not a limited vocal range; keep an eye out for this tendency if you are a composer that does not sing.

Writing Prompt #4

For this exercise:

1. Determine which type of melody writer best describes you: step, rhythmic, or intervallic.

2. Then, select a lyric that has no music written for it yet.

3. Tease out a rhythm implied by the lyric that feels natural to you. Write an original melody to that lyric by choosing two or three writing options offered in this chapter and what seems to work best for the internal rhythm and cadence of the lyric.

Write your melody so:

- It develops step, rhythmic, and intervallic motion across the song form.

- The pitch of your melody rises in the register across the song form.

- It starts the verse melody with step-wise motion.

- It adds more rhythmic motion in the prechorus.

- It adds all three elements of step, rhythmic, and intervallic motion in the chorus

8

Points of View

Writing with and from the Point of View of Objects, Values, Elements, Products, Animals, and Time

Writing songs from the point of view of objects: a train in Steve Goodman's "The City of New Orleans"; a product/beverage, as in Brad Paisley's "Alcohol"; or from the perspective of a value in Jamie O'Hara's "The Cold Hard Truth" and Billy Yates's use of values in "Choices," gives writers a unique opportunity for creative expression.

Objects tie us to time, places, events, memories, and emotions: the ring handed down from grand-mother to mother to daughter, the seashells in a winter coat pocket found a year later and placed there by an ex-girlfriend for safekeeping—they remain, she's gone.

Objects can be used to make a case for one's hopes or beliefs, as in Gary Burr's "Can't Be Really Gone" or Sting's "Message in a Bottle," or to confirm the outcome of a lifetime of behaviors, as in "The Cold Hard Truth" or "The Future You'll Never Have."

The matching of story line to environment to the need for emotional expression are endless; the potential for originality, high.

Objects represent milestones and everyday occurrences in our lives. Unique personal details of our stories can be told with and through them. We know images are sticky and statements are less so, so writing with objects gives writers a bit of a double bump.

This is especially true when the kindling fueling these stories are emotions of longing, missed opportunity, alienation, or the desire to connect with someone or something missed or cherished.

Writing in the present creates an undeniable need in an audience to listen in the present. The technique of writing a song where the singer is standing at a crossroads and must choose to turn either left or right in that moment is a powerful invitation for an audience to listen. "Issues," performed by Julia Michaels, is a good example (her issue being: grappling with trading her independence for dependence on another, making her vulnerable to the new demands of intimacy).

When real suffering or real relief will come from making the right or wrong decision in the moment, the stakes are high. Add honesty, good visual storytelling, craft, a mix of strong melody, performance, and/or production, and your song is on a collision course with millions of hearts who want to press Play and listen over and over again.

Good songwriting operates on so many levels at once, weaving together strands of need, intention, emotion, history, craft, storytelling, images, metaphor, simile, allegory, analogy, melody, music, arrangement, sound, and more.

Creative Uses of Objects in Songwriting: "Message in a Bottle"

Sting's "Message in a Bottle" is a great example of a song that uses an object to express loneliness, alienation, longing, and human connectivity. Critique it across the song form with your new craft tools and appreciate the mix of creativity, wisdom, and raw musical alchemy that went into writing it.

"Message in a Bottle" ▶

by Gordon Sumner (Sting)

> Just a castaway
> An island lost at sea
> Another lonely day
> With no one here but <u>me</u>
> More loneliness
> Than any man could bear
> <u>Rescue</u> me before I fall into despair

The first four opening lines use pictures to tell us where the singer is and what/why he's singing the song. No guesswork, and a little poetry thrown in too (an island lost at sea)! The song is about loneliness.

The next three lines SUM UP the verse by spelling out what's at stake for the narrator, and SETS UP the downbeat of the chorus.

I'll send an SOS to the world

I'll send an SOS to the world

I hope that someone gets my

Message in a bottle

> The first two lines of the chorus are ACTION LINES. The lyrics show action with a picture and then use repetition. The last two lines are a statement followed by a picture: the song's title!

A year has passed since I wrote my note

But I should have known this right from the start

Only hope can keep me together

Love can mend your life

But love can break your heart

> Adding time show the stakes are getting higher; the narrator's despair is growing. This new information fuels the song's momentum and spells out/harvests more of the song's DNA.

I'll send an SOS to the world

I'll send an SOS to the world

I hope that someone gets my

Message in a bottle

> Adding a bit of wisdom—love can heal but also break your heart— is always good in songs!

Walked out this morning

Don't believe what I saw

A hundred billion bottles

Washed up on the shore

Seems I'm not alone at being alone

A hundred billion castaways

Looking for a home

> Good songs add momentum, weight, and relevance with each part of the song form. Sting does this in the third verse by going from the micro—one person's experience—to the macro—bringing the entire world into the song; it's everyone's story now!

I'll send an SOS to the world

I'll send an SOS to the world

I hope that someone gets my

Message in a bottle

Sending out an SOS

Here's what Sting wrote about the song:

> "Message in a Bottle," is a good song that can move me. I like the idea that while it's about loneliness and alienation it's also about finding solace and other people going through the same thing.
>
> The guy's on a desert island and throws a bottle out to sea saying he's alone and all these millions of bottles come back saying, So what So am I! I like the fact that the whole deal is clinched by the third verse. It makes a journey. —Sting, Q, November 1993

📍 Creative GPS Critique of "Message in a Bottle"

🧠 Song Intention

To let the world know of a man's loneliness, despair, and alienation and his hope to be saved by a call for help

😨 Core Emotion

Hope

🎵 Song Category

Personal alienation/a cry for salvation

👥 Audience Tracking

- First-person story song

- The use of time progression, first verse to second verse

- Dropping a bit of wisdom on us in verse 2, adding great momentum and weight:

  "But I should have known this right from the start
  Only hope can keep me together
  Love can mend your life
  But love can break your heart"

- From personal story in verses 1 and 2 to everybody's story, verse 3

Writing with Objects in Service of Hope: "Can't Be Really Gone" and Make Me Laugh"

What do we want to happen from singing our song? Knowing the What? of the story, tied to using objects, allows the writer to get way ahead of the audience to create a unique landscape for the listener to enter, one that's both surprising and familiar.

Gary Burr's "Can't Be Really Gone" uses the building blocks of objects very differently from "Message in a Bottle," revealing an entirely different and unique way to use them. By taking everyday objects in the environment, he builds a case for remaining hopeful a breakup is repairable. The heavy elements flying off this collision between the reality and hope are loss, but lighter metals, such as folly and foolishness, follow.

Hindsight is 20/20, but combining memories of places visited with (her) objects lying around their home, a home that is no more (due to "The errors of his ways") makes the song truly heartbreaking. There are big dividends paid for originality, honesty, craft, and memorability. "Can't Be Really Gone" has those in spades. Fellow songwriters, here's a great example to follow to write a truly original song of loss and hope.

"Can't Be Really Gone" ▶

by Gary Burr

> Her hat is hanging by the door
> The one she bought in Mexico
> It blocked the wind, it stopped the rain
> She'd never leave that one
> So, she can't be really gone
>
> The shoes she bought on Christmas Eve
> She laughed and said they called her name
> It's like they're waiting in the hall
> For her to slip them on
> So, she can't be really gone

I don't know when she'll come back

She must intend to come back

And I've seen the error of my ways

Don't waste the tears on me

What more proof do you need

Just look around the room

So much of her remains

Her book is lying on the bed

The Two of Hearts to mark her page

Now, who could ever walk away

At chapter twenty-one

So, she can't be really gone

Just look around the room

So much of her remains

Her book is lying on the bed

The Two of Hearts to mark her page

Now, who could ever walk away

With so much left undone

So, she can't be really gone

No, she can't be really gone

⚲ Creative GPS Critique of "Can't Be Really Gone"

⬙ Song Intention

The singers need to persuade themselves a lost love will come back to them

⬙ Core Emotions

Hope, regret

♬ Song Category

Breakup song

⬙ Audience Tracking

- The use of third person: "her," and "she" establishes the singer as the narrator.

- Visual storytelling with objects: The audience sees these objects/details and can relate deeply to them because they possess them too.

- The lyric payoff established in each verse is tied to song form.

- The song is a Tag Line Song, making the entire song a chorus (with a refrain or bridge)

Other interesting craft usage in "Can't Be Really Gone" are:

- The song is written in the moment. This equals urgency to the listener, and there's no substitute for getting a song into the bloodstream of your audience faster than you singing or writing your song in the moment from the perspective of the moment you've realized the impact of the emotions you're feeling.

- The pictures (the very personal details) build the case for the statement embodied in the song title. The logic and order of each line is clear and builds momentum and payoff.

- The prime emotion driving the song is hope. He hopes she's coming back. We know what's at stake for the singer: the future of his relationship with a woman he loves. The appeal to anyone who's been, at this point, in a failing relationship to find the slimmest ray of hope is also a big factor in keeping us, the audience, involved deeply with the song.

- The subtext emotion is regret. He says he has "seen the errors of his ways," in the bridge or refrain. We know why he's singing the song: he regrets his actions.

- He let the audience put their life in the song! It's important that we don't know what he did, so we can substitute our own "errors of (our) ways" into the song, as listeners

- Repetition: Each stanza is a laundry list of her belonging. These details tell a visual story.

- It's a "Tag Line Song" meaning he tags the title on to the end of each stanza. This song form acts or make the entire song a chorus with a refrain or bridge. A very smart use of craft!

In "Make Me Laugh," the singer's bittersweet lament is for the warmth of a flame that burns no more, a past love that once brought fulfillment. Let's look at how using objects and other mechanics employed propel the song forward.

"Make Me Laugh" ▶

by Billy Seidman

> I let your memory take me back
> To the time you made me laugh
> It's been so long since we lost track
> And you could always make me laugh
>
> I found a faded rose in a birthday card
> A smiley face you drew with stars
> A book marked with our photograph
> From back when you could make me laugh
>
> Oh seems no one compares to you
> And I may live a lifetime
> Finding out that's true
>
> I took a walk last night down by the shore
> And watched the stars they shine no more
> Seems my life's been torn in half
> Since back when you could make me laugh
> Ooh

Listen to "Make Me Laugh" at: https://www.broadjam.com/songs/billyseidman/make-me-laugh-ingenue

📍 Creative GPS: Critique of "Make Me Laugh"

🧠 Song Intention

Found objects lead to reminiscing about a past lover and bittersweet memories.

😵 Core Emotion

Loss, regret

🎵 Song Category

Breakup song

👥 Audience Tracking

- Singing directly to "you" brings/invites the audience immediately into the song.

- An intimate detail of someone making us laugh is a deeply happy memory, tied to loss (the use of lyrical contrast).

- Using a Tag Line Song form helps turn the entire song lyric into a story, hook, chorus.

- The Summing Up of letting "Your memory take me back" sets up the double use of the Genesis line of the song in the first stanza and then the specific event: finding a faded rose in the second stanza.

- The bridge speaks a hard truth about "the one that got away," and everybody has someone who is "the one that got away"

Other interesting craft usage in "Make Me Laugh" are:

- The song title/the song idea does the heavy lifting! The use of pictures, images, and objects (the very personal details of roses, birthday cards, books, and photographs) build the case for the statement made in the song title. The logic and order of each line are clear, build momentum, and pay off with new energy each time the title is sung.

- Again, the song's written in the moment. Writing in the moment equals urgency to the listener, and there's no substitute for getting a song into the bloodstream of your audience faster than your singing or writing your song in the moment from the perspective of the moment you've realized the impact of the emotions you're feeling.

- Song Form: Both this song and "Can't Be Really Gone" are Tag Line Songs: the title comes at the "tag," or end, of each stanza (making each stanza feel like a whole chorus).

- The prime emotion driving the song is celebrating/remembering a once deep love. The warmth of caring memories meets bittersweet and flat-out sad, evoking a strong emotional reaction.

- The subtext emotion is acceptance: The singer may never find a love that compares to her/him, that's what's at stake for the singer, the singer's future happiness. There is no going back and fixing this; it's real. That's life, and though painful, people appreciate the honesty. The song stands up to the BS detector test, a big factor in keeping the audience involved deeply with the song. Their attention will disperse as soon as they detect artificiality.

- The audience has been invited to see their life in the song. The pictures and details represent objects we all often get from people who care about us.

- Happy melody/music, sad lyric.

- Repetition: Each stanza is a laundry list of remembrances, the details of which tell a visual story.

Writing from the Point of View of a Value: "The Cold Hard Truth" and "Lie"

"The Cold Hard Truth" is a song sung from the point of view of a value. The authority that gives a singer/songwriter is heady and thrilling. Speaking hard truths through the voice of a narrator creates an opportunity to give an unvarnished appraisal of love, life, and choices made. Jamie O'Hara's song is a great example of this art and craft in action.

"The Cold Hard Truth" ▸

by Jamie O'Hara

> You don't know who I am
> But I know all about you
> I've come to talk to you tonight
> About the things I've seen you do
>
> I've come to set the record straight
> I've come to shine the light on you
> Let me introduce myself
> I'm the cold hard truth
>
> There is a woman we both know
> I think you know the one I mean
> She gave her heart and soul to you
> You gave her only broken dreams
>
> You say your not the one to blame
> For all the heartaches she's been through
> I say you're nothing but a liar
> And I'm the cold hard truth

(BRIDGE)

All your life that's how it's been

Lookin' out for number one

Takin' more than you give

Movin' on when you're done

With her you could have had it all

A family and love to last

If you had any sense at all

You'd go and beg her to come back

You think that you're a real man

But you're nothing but a fool

The way you run away from love

The way you try to play it cool

I'm gonna say this just one time

Time is running out on you

You best remember me my friend

I am the cold hard truth.

You best remember me my friend

I am the cold hard truth.

⦿ Creative GPS: Critique of "The Cold Hard Truth"

☻ Song Intention

To persuade a selfish man he has one last chance to change his ways and find true love

☻☻ Core Emotions

Guilt, selfishness, fear, hope

♫ Song Category

Authority Song, breakup song, life lesson

☷ Audience Tracking

- The authority of the songs narrator is a surprise and is established in the first verse; that gets our attention. The second verse immediately starts a story, telling us what the song's about, and why we should listen.

- Intimate details: By the second verse, we know what's at stake for the characters: she gave her heart and soul and he, in return, gave her broken dreams.

- The use of time comes into the song in the bridge "All your life"

I had seen Jamie O'Hara perform this song at the Bluebird Café in Nashville many years ago; it made a strong impression. A dozen or so years later, a conversation, an "event," caused me to think about writing a song that took the opposite side of the truth; the result was "Lie."

"Lie"

by Billy Seidman

> I'm the check in the mail
> The sure thing that can't fail
> I'm your ship about to come in
>
> I'm the promise you'll call her
> The heels that make you taller
> I'm the pledge to stop drinking again
>
> I come in all sizes I'm usually white
> But grow black as a tornado sky
>
> Fishermen spin me
> I'm a guilty man's first plea
> Who am I, I'm a lie
>
> A car salesman sold me
> George Washington never told me
> I'm the reason we invaded Iraq
>
> I'm why Elvis ain't dead
> Why Gold's made from lead
> Why they walk like a duck but don't quack
>
> When there's way too much month at the end of the money
> I'm the excuse when the landlord asks why

I'm the dog ate my homework

A bald man's comb-over

I'm dye, yeah I'm a lie

(BRIDGE)

I sounded good on the playground

So good that I stayed around

Through high school then college then life

I'm a genuine fake make the truth a mistake

To the ears of your boss or your wife

The funny thing is the more that you tell me

The harder it is to feel right

Like a horse to a plow you're use to me now

Let me fly, I'm a lie

(TAG)

I'm the big idea when you're high

The divorce where the ink never dries

The stutter when you're getting tongue-tied

Who am I, I'm a lie, I'm a lie, and I'm a lie . . .

Readers are encouraged to write their own Creative GPS critique of "Lie," and post it at info@ songartsacademy.com.

The preface to the *Elements* referenced this next song. Its title, the use of objects, and the vignette strategy used to write it play well together, and so it's included for critiquing and review here.

"A Circle Has No Sides" ▶

by Billy Seidman

> I wish I was more like a mountain
> So I could rise above it all
> I'd be solid and strong as granite
> And clouds would seem so small
>
> Wish I was more like the wind
> I'd soar where Eagles fly
> Wish I was more like a circle
> Cause a circle has no sides
>
> Wish I was just like a river
> I'd flow so easily
> I'd know just where I was headed
> I'd be a part of a great big sea
>
> Wish I was just like a desert
> Where horizons are so wide
> Wish I was more like a circle
> Cause a circle has no sides
>
> (CHORUS)
> A circle has no sides
> So why oh why should you or I
> A circle has no sides
> So why do you and I

Isn't what we have in common
So much stronger than our pride
Let's be more like a circle
A circle has no sides

I know the day is coming though it may take a million years
Where people will learn to think before they act in fear
Where no one's gonna know of words like conquer or divide
And fulfillment comes when your neighbor's done just as well as you and I

(CHORUS)

(TAG)
Oh join me in this circle of light, A circle has no sides

Readers are encouraged to write their own Creative GPS critique of "A Circle Has No Sides," and post it at info@songartsacademy.com.

Writing from the Point of View of a Product/Beverage: "Alcohol"

Brad Paisley's "Alcohol" (note: a single-word title) is flat out awesome, a superfun entertainment and "drinking" song. He found a unique, honest, and picturesque way to own the word and write a song that's gonna last . . .

"Alcohol" ▶

by Brad Paisley

> I can make anybody pretty
> I can make you believe any lie
> I can make you pick a fight
> With somebody twice your size
>
> Well I've been known to cause a few breakups
> And I've been known to cause a few births
> I can make you new friends
> Or get you fired from work
>
> (CHORUS)
> And since the day I left Milwaukee
> Lynchburg, Bordeaux, France
> Been making the bars
> With lots of big money
> And helping white people dance
>
> I got you in trouble in high school
> And college now that was a ball
> You had some of the best times
> You'll never remember with me
> Alcohol, Alcohol

I got blamed at your wedding reception
For your best man's embarrassing speech
And also for those naked pictures of you at the beach

I've influenced kings and world leaders
I helped Hemingway write like he did
And I'll bet you a drink or two that I can make you
Put that lampshade on your head

(CHORUS)

And since the day I left Milwaukee
Lynchburg, Bordeaux, France
Been making a fool
out of folks Just like you
And helping white people dance
I am medicine and I am poison
I can help you up or make you fall
You had some of the best times
You'll never remember with me
Alcohol, alcohol

(CHORUS)

Readers are encouraged to write their own Creative GPS critique of "Alcohol" and post it at info@ songartsacademy.com.

Writing from the Point of View of an Animal: "You're My Everything"

Frank Marr, a former student wrote, "You're My Everything" as an assignment in one of my workshops. The song's cleverness, heart, honesty, and originality support the premise "a great idea does the heavy lifting in songwriting." Frank's song remains a favorite.

Written from the point of view of his girlfriend's dog, we learn exactly what's at stake for the little guy.

"You're My Everything" ▶

by Frank Marr

> Mama, when you coming home?
> 'Cause I don't do so well alone
> Smother me with everything you've got
> 'Cause I can't get enough love
>
> Grr . . . Hey stranger! You better stay the fuck away
> I may be small but I will save the day
> I'm always looking out, 'cause I'm the man of the house
> And I can't get enough
>
> (CHORUS)
> I want, I want, I want, I want more
> Gimme, gimmie, gimmie, gimmie more
> I want, I want, I want to be your everything
> You're my everything

My leg's shaking in the air

You hit my spot again

And I don't suspect that this will ever end

But oh no! You went away

And I still wanna play

'Cause I can't get enough

(CHORUS)

(BRIDGE)

And when you say I am bad

I don't understand it

I must have ruined everything

And just at the moment that we lost all we had

there you are And it's ok

And I can't get enough

(CHORUS)

And I got to be sure

I'm your everything

Listen to "You're My Everything" at: https://soundcloud.com/frankmarr/sets/songartsacademy

Readers are encouraged to write their own Creative GPS critique of "You're My Everything" and post it at info@songartsacademy.com.

Writing from the Point of View of Time: "The Future You'll Never Have"

The future knows everything; it is the ultimate authority; it can pass stinging judgement or bestow compassion. What does the future have to say about someone who's made bad decision after bad decision ending up far from where they'd hope to be?

"The Future You'll Never Have"

by Billy Seidman

> I watched you walk out of the water
> While your brother cried for help
> When strangers pulled him from the surf
> You thought only of yourself
>
> Now you're sure that he still trusts you
> But I can see the truth from here
> He's loses faith in you with every passing year
> And you ask me how I know that it's that bad
> I'm the future you'll never have
>
> You dream a lavish lifestyle
> But you never have the cash
> Never had ethic or ambition
> To make the vision come to pass
> Think you'll trade up from your basement
> To an east side penthouse pad
> Woah, that's never gonna happen
> I'm the future you'll never have

(REFRAIN)

I'm the spring that would have blossomed
In the beat of every heart
Of each girl who tried to love you
But you never gave enough
I'm the turn you should have taken
At the fork in every road
You'll be just a step from happy 'stead of sad
Reads the letter returned to sender
From the future you'll never have

In every cloud's a silver lining
Between each shadow there's a light
Where you should take a little comfort
Before guessing wrong or right

But you bargained with the devil
And my contract's ironclad
You signed away the joy of living
To the Future you'll never have

(REFRAIN)

Writing Prompt #5

Write a song from either:

- The point of view of an object (or living thing other than a person)

- A value

- A product

- The elements (wind, rain, light, etc.)

- Or use objects to justify a belief you hold

Critique the song form of a few songs in this genre for clues to how best set up and write the song. Use all the applicable craft tools in *The Elements* to critique your song under construction, to ensure you're building a strong song for you to sing and an audience to listen to.

9

Inspiration

Average Is Your Enemy

Make every note and word fight for its right to exist in your songs.

Competition

It may register as less than a "kumbaya" moment to start a chapter on inspiration by addressing competition, but it's relevant as the world's entertainment marketplace is flooded with songwriters vying for attention.

Your songs, your voice, your unique style of bringing the world into your world, your vision, then holding its attention so an audience willingly comes back for more, becomes a fan, then spreads the news about you—all are subject to competition and the clock.

Confusing Quality Singing for Quality Songs

It's all too common that performers who are exceptional singers confuse the applause they get as being for their songwriting. The standard for great singer-songwriters is to especially excel at songwriting. This is a trap developing singer-songwriters can fall into: coasting on vocal and performance chops while forgoing the vigilance and craft needed to write songs of immense power when you've already got an audience marveling at your delivery system: your voice or stage presence.

A reality check on your vocal prowess versus your songwriting will lead to writing better songs and a longer career.

Aiming high with a song's aspiration and successfully pulling off that feat of emotional hypnotic alchemy is the standard of success in songwriting and live performance (the perfect measurement of topic and emotion translated to melody, lyrics, intention, and sound/production).

If you're *not* pulling it off, the audience, discreetly or not, disengages: they text, chat, and move on to the next songwriter . . .

"Average is your enemy," says Bob Doyle, a respected music executive in Nashville and New York. Typically everyone assumes that it's the other guy that's average, not them . . .

The truth seems to be somewhere between extremes. No one arrives fully formed. How one finds, then marries inspiration to craft seems to be the hedge in creating authenticity and originality in songwriting.

Honesty and Growth

It's worth noting that Ray Charles didn't become Ray Charles overnight; one of his first commercial identities was as a Nat King Cole knockoff. The level of honesty needed to look deep in the mirror—past all the encouragement received for years from parents, family, friends and colleagues—to ask how good or original you really are, is a terrifying but necessary place to create real growth. Growth that leads to harnessing the themes that resonate deepest, those "shape of your heart" themes that are the life source used to create songs of lasting power, relevance, and beauty.

Another way to think of growth is the ability to learn and keep learning. This is the template for the songwriting athlete: the everyday use of song craft builds perception (through writing hundreds of songs), which forms the core strength, core muscle in songwriting. Having this muscle, this depth of perception, is the goal.

Your new songwriting mantra: to be fully present in the moment to witness the emotional transactions happening around you every day, then reporting back to us, your audience, what you saw that everyone else missed.

Peer into those tiny emotional cracks that wandering the world with a present heart opens. Your sensitivity to them snowballs into opportunity to write impossibly creative and original songs. That's how your songwriting heroes did and do it, and so will you.

Capture those "what's at stake for someone else" moments that you witness which subjectively and shockingly lead back to seeing what's truly at stake for you.

That connection with something so personal, something we didn't quite understand the depth of before, sparks a revelation, and when composed with the masterful use of craft, makes for songs we need to write, and thereby, the world needs to hear.

This cycle of honesty and achievement was made possible due to the presence your Songwriting Athleticism™ built (by your tenacious commitment to be a better songwriter every day for years).

You can say with certainty the great songwriters past and present are much like UN ambassadors to the human heart: they represent everyone's hopes, desires, fears, joys, and struggles in their songs. They understand because they learned how to look into their own heart first.

Are you up for that? Looking into your own heart that deeply?

Writing songs that can touch and change the lives of everyone who hears them? Aiming that high in your ambition?

Are you ready to take this kind of personal journey of discovery, honesty, urgency, and craft them into songs? It's the right question to ask because you'll need this vision, or something like it, to supply and sustain your own encouragement during the process of getting better until you're ready to write some of the best songs of your life.

These are challenges not mentioned in the songwriters' "Hallmark Card" moments, or handbook, or career guide. The music side of songwriting can nourish your soul. The business side of it can break your heart and spirit.

Yes, you can "make a killing" in it, but it's near impossible to make a living at it for the thousands upon thousands that try each year.

All the more reason to get good and not kid yourself about what good, great, and brilliant songwriting is—as well as what's fair, bad, and plain awful songwriting. Keep your ears attuned for identifying the entire spectrum of awful to brilliant in every song you hear or write.

The Muse: Standing on the Shoulders of Giants

"If you aim for the stars, at least you're not coming back with a handful of mud." —anonymous

If you're fortunate to attend the annual Songwriters Hall of Fame Awards Ceremony, you might witness the presentation of its Towering Song Award.

The award recognizes the achievement of originality and emotional connection great songs continuously make with audiences over time. "Moon River," Fly Me to the Moon," and "Bridge over Troubled Water" are a few of the songs commemorated by the Hall of Fame as Towering Songs.

Who are your heroes of song? What Towering Songs have they written that touch and inspire you to aim higher?

Study them well, aim to best their best, at the very least, and come to understand the mechanics of how they were written, so in your songwriting career you'll know what to ask the muse to grace you with.

"The Song Remembers When"

Hugh Prestwood's "The Song Remembers When" is, to me, a personal towering song for a host of reasons, primarily because he saw something everybody else missed but him, then turned what he saw/felt into a massive original idea for a song that has stood up and lasted. Listen, review, and critique it:

"The Song Remembers When" ▶

by Hugh Prestwood

I was standing at the counter
I was waiting for the change
When I heard that old familiar music start
It was like a lighted match had been tossed into my soul
It was like a dam had broken in my heart

After taking every detour
Gettin' lost and losin track
So that even if I wanted I could not find my way back
After driving out the memory
Of the way things might have been
After I'd forgotten all about us
The song remembers when

We were rolling through the Rockies
We were up above the clouds
When a station out of Jackson played that song
And it seemed to fit the moment
And the moment seemed to freeze
When we turned the music up and sang along

And there was a God in Heaven
And the world made perfect sense
We were young and were in love
And we were easy to convince

We were headed straight for Eden
It was just around the bend
And though I have forgotten all about it
The song remembers when

I guess something must have happened
And we must have said goodbye
And my heart must have been broken
Though I can't recall just why
The song remembers when

Well, for all the miles between us
And for all the time that's past
You would think I haven't gotten very far
And I hope my hasty heart
Will forgive me just this once
If I stop to wonder how on earth you are

But that's just a lot of water
Underneath a bridge I burned
And there's no use in backtracking
Around corners I have turned
Still I guess some things we bury
Are just bound to rise again
Yeah, and even if the whole world has forgotten
The song remembers when

"Goodbye Yellow Brick Road"

Now apply your critiquing skills to the "modern Mozart" of pop melody writing, Sir Elton John and his collaborator Bernie Taupin's "Goodbye Yellow Brick Road."

"Goodbye Yellow Brick Road" ▶

by Elton John and Bernie Taupin

> When are you gonna come down?
> When are you going to land?
> I should have stayed on the farm
> I should have listened to my old man
>
> You know you can't hold me forever
> I didn't sign up with you
> I'm not a present for your friends to open
> This boy's too young to be singing, the blues
>
> So goodbye yellow brick road
> Where the dogs of society howl
> You can't plant me in your penthouse
> I'm going back to my plough
>
> Back to the howling old owl in the woods
> Hunting the horny back toad
> Oh I've finally decided my future lies
> Beyond the yellow brick road
>
> What do you think you'll do then?
> I bet that'll shoot down your plane
> It'll take you a couple of vodka and tonics
> To set you on your feet again

Maybe you'll get a replacement

There's plenty like me to be found

Mongrels who ain't got a penny

Sniffing for tidbits like you on the ground

So goodbye yellow brick road

Where the dogs of society howl

You can't plant me in your penthouse

I'm going back to my plough

Back to the howling old owl in the woods

Hunting the horny back toad

Oh I've finally decided my future lies

Beyond the yellow brick road

Songs That Contrast Musical and Lyrical Intent

Follow the Tears

This is an entire category of song that employs writing *bright, sing-song melodies, married to darker lyrical content*. A few songs from this set include:

- "Alone Again (Naturally)"

- "But Not for Me"

- James Taylor's "Sunny Skies"

- Bryan White's "Someone Else's Star"

"Alone Again (Naturally)"

Apply your critiquing skills to uncover the engines driving Gilbert O'Sullivan's subversive and masterful, "Alone Again (Naturally)."

"Alone Again (Naturally)" ▸

written and performed by Gilbert O'Sullivan

> In a little while from now
>
> If I'm not feeling any less sour
>
> I promise myself to treat myself
>
> And visit a nearby tower
>
> And climbing to the top will throw myself off
>
> In an effort to make it clear to who
>
> Ever what it's like when you're shattered
>
> Left standing in the lurch at a church
>
> Where people saying: "My God, that's tough
>
> She's stood him up"
>
> No point in us remaining
>
> We may as well go home
>
> As I did on my own
>
> Alone again, naturally
>
> To think that only yesterday
>
> I was cheerful, bright and gay
>
> Looking forward to well wouldn't do
>
> The role I was about to play
>
> But as if to knock me down
>
> Reality came around
>
> And without so much, as a mere touch
>
> Cut me into little pieces
>
> Leaving me to doubt

Talk about God and His mercy

Or if He really does exist

Why did He desert me in my hour of need

I truly am indeed Alone again, naturally

It seems to me that there are more hearts

broken in the world that can't be mended

Left unattended

What do we do? What do we do?

Alone again, naturally

Now looking back over the years

And whatever else that appears

I remember I cried when my father died

Never wishing to hide the tears

And at sixty-five years old

My mother, God rest her soul,

Couldn't understand why the only man

She had ever loved had been taken

Leaving her to start with a heart so badly broken

Despite encouragement from me

No words were ever spoken

And when she passed away

I cried and cried all day

Alone again, naturally

Alone again, naturally

Why does this potentially depressing, self-indulgent song connect so deeply and personally with listeners? The common denominators found in "Alone Again (Naturally)" and others on the list include:

- Heartbreak and loss

- The song form: They are not in the traditional ABABCB (verse, chorus, verse, chorus, bridge, chorus) form. They fall more typically into the (AACA) song form where the title is "tagged onto" the end of each verse or refrain.

- They have extremely memorable repetitive melody-motifs at their musical core.

- They are not in minor keys! Although these songs express intense feelings of personal loss, the choice of the writers to not make them musically "dark" or moody is, I believe, a key to their great success.

- The urgency/need to write the songs: Somehow in an instinctive, barely perceivable way, the listener begins to sense the singer is strong enough to express these emotions. Somehow the singer seems to be benefiting, perhaps even healing, through the act of singing.

- They have a great midtempo feel.

This act, this public transformation of the singer (and thereby the audience), is one of the highest achievements in songwriting.

Writing Prompt #6

Write a "follow the tears" song and make us love it!

- Use your urgency, your need to express it.

- Write personal lyrics; they can be dark or deep, but contrast them with a bright major key.

- Use a good midtempo beat/feel.

- Contrast these ingredients and serve us up something that is both emotionally revealing about you and musically compelling for the listener.

- Write it as a Tag Line Song, as in the song form of "Alone Again (Naturally)" or "She's Always a Woman to Me."

- Strive to make every line in your song matter; make a difference and build momentum to make your song title pay off richer each time it's sung.

- Use the full real estate value of each line to say what you mean and mean what you say.

- Use a good balance of images and statements.

What matters is that we hear/feel your need to write the song.

10
Rewriting Strategies

Great writers are critical of their own work, they have the courage to be critical,
to risk feeling inadequate to the task of making their work stronger.
They get to work and solve the problem.
—Jimmy Webb

Replacing Thinking with Feeling

A good rewrite takes all the thinking out of a song and replaces it with feeling.

Consider every song heard on radio, Spotify, film, broadcast television, cable, or in a TV or radio advertisement has been highly vetted. It's been written, rewritten, changed and adapted lyrically, musically, and track-wise many times over before it finds its way to our ears.

A listener typically hears the tail end of a long, exhaustive process to get the song and production where it needed to be.

For songwriters, the takeaway is: rewriting make for stronger songs, period!

What's qualifies as stronger? More memorable, honest, hookier, a more emotional satisfying and visually connected song. A shorter song, a song where any choice musically or lyrically that adds drag to the songs momentum has been removed. A very well-written song.

Personally, I don't care how many rewrites it takes—three to thirteen or more to get all the wood on the ball—until I arrive at that satisfied place where, in my head and heart, the song is finished. (Another strong reason to make sure you have a ball/idea worth hitting out of the park!)

Song lovers love bragging about a standout line in a song, a line that was either devastatingly honest, poetic, wise, funny, surprising, original, painful, joyous, full of sass, swagger, and attitude, or plain snarky. It's part of your job as a songwriter to come up with those standout lines, no matter how impossible it seems. Gaining experience as a rewriter is part of training to write such iconic lines or titles as:

- "The fundamental things apply as time goes by"

- "God bless the child that's got his own"

- "Hello darkness, my old friend"

- "Old enough to know better, still too young to care"

- "And in the end, the love you take is equal to the love you make"

- "Freedom's just another word for nothing left to lose"

- "You better start swimming or sink like a stone, cause the times they are a-changin'"

- "A writer takes his pen to write the words again all in love is fair"

- "The future's so bright, I gotta wear shades"

- "If we weren't all crazy we would go insane"

- "No Shoes No Shirt No Problem"

- "It's been a hard day's night"

- "I think it's about forgiveness even if you don't love me anymore"

- "There were so many people you just had to meet without your clothes and everybody knows"

Sometimes those lines pop into our head more often. It's a by-product of going deep and spending a lot of time fishing for them.

Staying in the Process

Leonard Cohen, known for his unique craftsmanship and work ethic, once said, "A song has to speak to me with a certain urgency. To find that song that I can be interested in, takes many versions and it takes a lot of uncovering."

Another phase attributed to Cohen that I often paraphrase is: "Often my first encounter with a song (idea) is my weakest." Cohen, like many brilliant writers, needed time to find out what his songs were ultimately about before he could properly finish them.

A geologist has a hunch based on rock samples, surveys, and scans that there are minerals in a search area, but it's the on-site digging that proves what's actually there. Our initial interest in an idea similarly just scratches the surface of its potential.

Once you've worked out your initial song draft, your musical or lyrical idea (not a notion), rewrites can lead to surprising places if you're willing and able to hang in there long enough to fully explore the terrain.

It's worth noting if you don't have the practice of redrafting songs three to ten times as part of your natural songwriting routine, you'll need to build up your stamina to become a strong rewriter.

That said, taking a break; a walk, clearing your mind, or a change of environment are also part of the rewrite process. A partial list of famous writers, all avid break takers and walkers, includes Aristotle, Beethoven, Charles Dickens, William Wordsworth, and Charles Darwin.

The point is to stay in the process; that's the secret weapon to songwriting success.

Even sleeping on an idea is staying in the process, as the unconscious mind keeps working on song rewrites, issues, or problems.

A pure inspiration can fuel a rewrite; a live performance of a stellar song by a stellar artist can often be a reminder of greatness and aiming high.

Sometimes, a melody's not developing enough contour or rhythm (hookiness) throughout the song form. Sometimes, one elusive lyric line is missing that would give the song its undeniable emotional center (its reason to exist and connect with listeners), or a second verse is too weak and needs to be stronger or even better written than the first verse.

These are the individual territorial gains, the inches scratched from the muse (or the lack of a muse) earned by staying in the process.

They are the moments to be most proud of your songwriting skills, in as they represent in action your maturity as a writer. You judged smartly what needed to be removed and what needed to be added; you sped up your storytelling by shrink-wrapping and summing up your lyrics; you gave space to a melody to let it breath and sink into the listeners heart before you rushed into the second verse. You spelled out in your bridge or refrain one last time why you wrote the song, what your root intention was.

All these decisions add momentum and fuel your song's march toward completion. The goal: a stronger song created by replacing thinking with feeling (your new rewrite mantra).

Sometimes, we face a seemingly Everest-like array of barriers to solving our song's puzzle, some due to the natural landscape of logistical challenges in pulling off an ambitious idea (an odd rhyme scheme or a key title word with very few rhyme options); at other times, the issues can be man-made (difference of opinions between collaborators as to what the song needs or what the song should sound like).

The Creation Space vs. the Rewrite Space

To simplify the process of uncovering what a song's "about," consider that there are two spaces in the songwriting process:

- The Creation Space

- The Rewrite space

In The Creation Space, we're focused on getting a toehold on a melody, chord progression, a track, a beat, a title, and words that flow in the general direction of our ideas, inspiration, and hopefully, lucky creative accidents.

Our frame and focus is on getting something going, not on scraping the excess glaze off the finish.

Lots of writers refer to a term "dare to suck": in The Creation Space, say out loud a line or anything else you deem relevant to say in a collaboration, as you just never know how or where an idea or line tossed into the ring or consciousness will lead to other ideas to emerge.

For experienced writers, the editorial process in The Creation Space is simple; they've written so many songs that the use of song craft is second nature. As a result, much of their songs editing/rewriting is already baked in to the process. (The song's been telling these experienced writers early in the process what it needs to be better written.)

For developing writers, The Creation Space can be an ocean of imagination with very few longitude and latitude lines to guide the song to a safe harbor.

The biggest hazard being thinking there is no hazard and your song's already done!

In practice, the rewrite space is where we assess and address how well a song's communicating our intention, then repair or massage the spots in need of more clarity, attitude, contrast, or any number of craft components the job calls for.

Listening, Reading, and Research

Simply said, the big rewrite tools are: listening, reading, and research.

Listen honesty to your work tape—recordings of your song under construction—many, many times over with a critical ear for what might make it stronger; read the lyrics, scanning them for opportunity, or contrast, or for what's generally weak or strong about them; then get to work on your next draft.

Research is key as in using dictionaries, thesauruses, rhyming dictionaries as well as Internet searches for songs that are similar, dissimilar, or just scanning for inspiration.

By this stage in *The Elements*, you've been exposed to a large toolkit of craft skills to critique and rewrite your songs with to be effective.

Also, take inspiration from your heroes of song. Their songs are examples of how high to aim in your songwriting ambitions. Although their best songs may seem unreachable as the top of Everest, remember that many started at a lowly base camp, as a writer with a kernel of inspiration staring at a blank sheet of paper or empty screen.

The takeaway: Your heroes of song used the rewrite space to figure out how to write it then write it better, so can you.

Common Mistakes and Fixes

Here's a list of what to listen for in the rewrite space related to *music* repairs, including

- Clearly hear what is causing drag on your song's momentum. Listen for any extra notes, notes that may have helped you write the original melody (in The Creation Space) but that, in the rewrite space, need to be removed because they're not allowing the melody to fully breathe, become more memorable, and more singable.

- Create enough musical contrast between parts of the song form.

- Don't start the second verse too soon after the last line of the chorus. Rushing the start of the second verse *prevents* the chorus line, song title, or tag line the time it needs to breathe, sink in, and have impact on the listener psyche.

- Often the tempo at which you wrote the song will most likely prove too slow for the final version. It was the right tempo in the creation space as your *hunt-and-peck* tempo to learn how the song went, but for the master recording, it will often be too slow.

- This can also be true of your song key. The original key felt natural to write it in, but may prove too high or too low for either you or someone else to sing on a master recording or master song demo. (Before recording a master or master demo, know the best key of the song for both male and female.)

- This holds true for accompaniment. That first guitar or piano part you came up with served you perfectly as a songwriter, but making a record of the song often demands that the accompanying part needs to change, as it may not fit within a more track-driven production arrangement (radio-friendly sounding or other approach). Be open and flexible in the rewrite accompaniment space; many options and a host of players can come into it and improve your songs chances for success.

- As mentioned prior, musical styles and sounds are constantly changing. You would not be the first writer on the way to a recording session to be inspired by the sound, textures, beat, emotion, or arrangement of a new (or old) song just heard on the radio challenging you to rewrite your song in some way to make it stronger on the spot.

Here's a list of what to listen and look for in the rewrite space related to lyric repairs, including:

- Reading/scanning for any extra words that were needed to write the song but, on review, are extraneous to the song's momentum. As simple as it may seem, even the use of the word *I* can be extraneous. Imagine in the song "Alfie" if the singer sang, "And I said, what's it all about, Alfie." (We know it's you singing the song; no need to say *I*.)

- Scanning your lyric for how *conversational* it is, is a smart use of time. Songs whose lyrics don't sound the way people actually talk everyday can sound pretentious and hollow.

- Notice when you are or are not applying the lyrical Opportunity, Perspective, Momentum, and Contrast tools (OPMC) discussed earlier in *The Elements*, as well as Creative GPS strategies, the SAA Critiquing Tool, and Title Ideation strategies to harvest all lyrical ideas imbedded in your song's DNA.

Removing Empty Calorie Words

Empty Calorie Words are descriptively empty or overused clichés. Words like *pain, love, it's, thing, this, something*, and *feeling* are typical Empty Calorie Words.

They beg the answer: What kind of *pain? love?* What kind of *it's? thing? something? feeling?* Empty Calorie Words merely point to a meaning; they're too general, too creatively lazy to typically have any lasting impact on a listener.

Although there are plenty examples of famous songs using words like *pain, love, thing, it's,* and so on, the distinction is to flag them for the opportunity to write up or improve one's visual storytelling by translating them to more definitive images or examples.

Empty Calorie Words may say what you mean, but they don't add color or originality. Writers should strive to find more in-depth images to replace them.

For example, if someone's constantly forty-five minutes late for a date you've made, don't opt for, "Guess *something's* not working" or "*It's* kinda strange." Writing that kind of line falls flat; it's a lost opportunity to build momentum and connect deeper with your audience.

Instead, try to deliver a specific, rich picture or detail, such as, "Guess the chairs on the table say you're not gonna show."

Writing Prompt #7

1. Go through a song you're currently working on and look for Empty Calorie Words.

2. Substitute any and all words that hint at details. Replace those words with action words that describe events.

3. Yes, you may have to adjust your musical phrasing to accommodate the new lyric, but this exercise is worth it. Why? Because now you're alerted to these empty words. If you stay alert and make this a common practice, in the next three, four, or five songs you write, Empty Calorie Words won't have any attraction for you anymore.

Once you've gotten good at replacing Empty Calorie Words, then—be my guest—go back to hinting all you want, because now *you have a choice* in the matter. My guess is that your taste buds will be hooked on a much richer creative diet.

Don't hint at the corners of ideas. Honest, direct, picture-driven images, details, and stories get the job done.

11

Protocol for Songwriters Working with Musicians

Chart Writing for Live and Studio Performances

Many successful songwriters are also some of the world's best musicians and producers.

As musicians, they've learned firsthand how often songwriters are ill prepared to articulate how they want their songs played or the kinds of musical parts a songwriter might want to hear live musicians and studio musicians create.

Rewriting charts while the clock is ticking (paying for those services), during rehearsals, live gigs, or in the studio is perhaps the biggest avoidable waste of time and money songwriters can navigate just by learning a few basic protocols musicians follow.

A few chart-writing techniques used to prepare for rehearsals, live performances, and recording session include the Nashville Number System and a standard musical notation–based chord chart (a.k.a. rhythm chart).

Both have their strengths. Let's look at the Nashville Number System first.

The Nashville Number System

"The Nashville Number System, or Number Chart, uses many common music conventions found in all written music; specifically direction signs, such as repeats, ending, or D.S. al coda.[1]

The system is based on taking each note in a scale and assigning it a number:

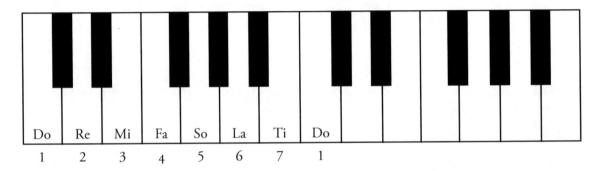

These numbers also represent chords built on each note of the scale. For example, in the key of C, the one chord is C, the 2 chord is D, and so forth.

Chord progressions are chord patterns created by moving these numbers around.

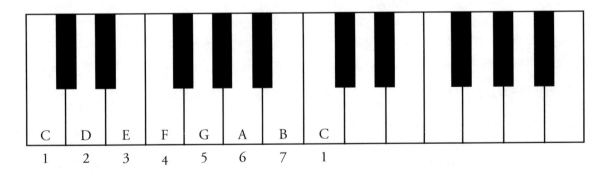

Your ear is already very familiar with many famous chord patterns. Your favorite songs are built on them; you just might not know they are interpreted or written this way.

---

1   "If you don't understand these, go ask your 3rd grade piano teacher. He or she will be happy to shame you for not continuing with your music studies." —Paul Scholten

Most popular music is based on creating variations of these numbers/chords to create chord progressions (chords built on each degree of the scale).

The chorus of John Denver's "Take Me Home, Country Roads," for example, looks like this:

5   1   5   6 minor   4

Take me Home Country Roads to the place I belong,

1   5   4   1

West Virginia, mountain mama, Take me home, country roads

If you play this song in the key of C, the corresponding chords to the numbers would be as follows:

G   C   G   A minor   F

Take me Home Country Roads to the place I belong,

C   G   F   C

West Virginia, mountain mama, Take me home, country roads

This is the simplest way to communicate to a musician the basic chord progression of your song. What's also great about the number system is it applies to all keys!

So, you *don't* have to write out a new chart (or add new numbers over lyrics) if you decide to raise or lower the key you sing a song in: 1 is 1 in all keys and for each scale degree. (There is no transposing of chord symbols to adjust for a key change in the number system.)

It's also a simple system to use if you want to play the song in both male and female keys. Typically a female key will be a fourth or fifth higher than a male key.

So for example, if the male sings the song comfortably in the key of C (C being the 1 chord in the key of C), then the female key will most likely be comfortable in the key of F (the fourth degree up from 1 in the C scale)

Although each number (each chord) can be a major, minor, seventh, sus (suspended; an added fourth) or diminished chord, for our purposes now (for simplicity's sake), let's just say each chord number has a *primary sound* that's either major or minor. For example in the key of C:

- The 1 is a major chord. C

- The 2 is a minor chord. D minor

- The 3 can be both. E minor—C/E

- The 4 is a major. F

- The 5 is major. G

- The 6 is minor. A minor

- The 7 is a half-diminished chord (a minor chord where the fifth is flatted). B half-diminished

- The 1 can also be an octave higher (the same sound as the first 1, but pitched an octave higher in the register).

Each of the these chords is used to create chord progressions, typically a series of three or four different chords played in succession that make up a verse, a prechorus, a chorus, and a bridge, for example.

If you're not a musician, no worries. You don't need to know how to play guitar or piano to help yourself put a chord progression together to play simple songs or for your original songs.

Try this exercise using "Take Me Home, Country Roads" as an example. All you need to know is how to locate the note middle C on a piano keyboard. Once you've done that:

1. Play the C and sing the C note, calling it 1, then play all the white keys and sing their proper number as you play them:

2. D = 2

3. E = 3

4. F = 4

5. G = 5

6. A = 6

7. B = 7

8. C = 1

Now that you understand how to sing the notes in the scale with the proper number, sing the melody to "Take Me Home, Country Roads" while playing the corresponding number above the words on the piano or keyboard:

5   1   5   6 minor   4

Take me Home Country Roads to the place I belong,

1   5   4   1

West Virginia, mountain mama, Take me home, country roads

With this simple knowledge, you can now use the number system to substitute for any chord for your original songs by playing these numbers under your melodies.

Why? Because the number of the chord also is the same as the bass note that supports your songs melody, so you don't need to actually play the full chord(s) to get your meaning across to a musician.

A more practiced musician will understand immediately what chords, or substitute chords, or passing notes can be used to make your song's accompaniment arrangement more musically interesting.

Here are number charts for both "Breakeven," and "Thinking Out Loud," written out as if top Nashville studio musicians were hired to record the songs.

Note: While reading the Nashville System Number charts, make mental notes of these particular details. They make for a clearer and concise road map of the song:

- An underlined set of numbers—for example, <u>4 5</u>—indicates a bar of 4/4 with two chords in it, with each chord having a value of two beats (two beats for the 4, and two beats for the 5 chord, in this example).

- An arrow above and to the right of a chord in a two-chord bar indicates that the second chord in that bar is pushed or anticipated. (This means the second chord is played on the "and 2," or +2 beat, of that bar. A bar of 4/4 time is counted in eighth notes as 1+2+3+4+.)

- Single dots above chords in a bar indicate quarter-note rhythms.

- Note the use of classical music notation for D.S., first and second endings, and D.S. al coda signs.

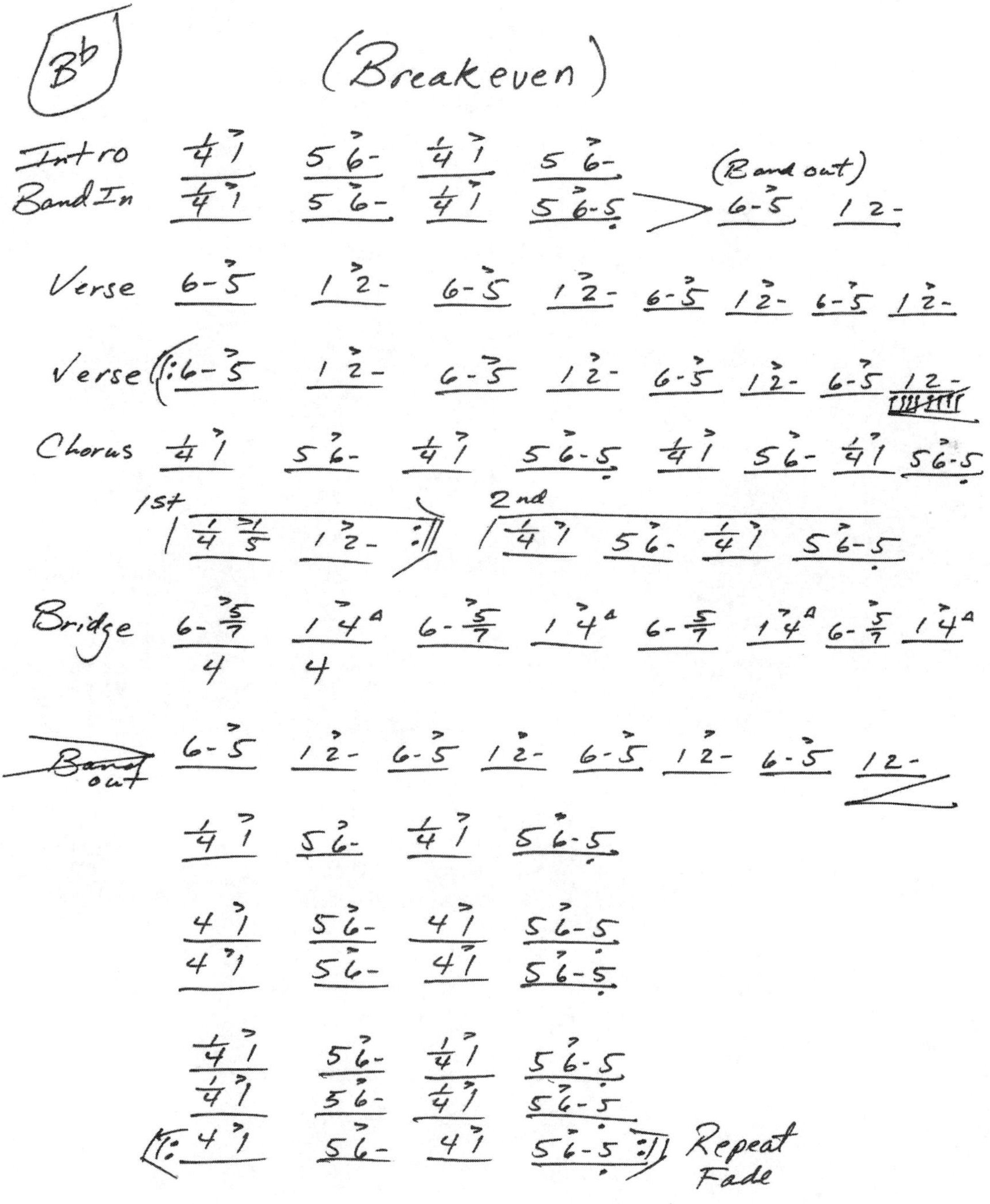
B♭
(Breakeven)
Intro
Band In
(Band out)
Verse
Verse
Chorus
1st
2nd
Bridge
Band out
Repeat
Fade

$(Breakeven)$
notes

$\boxed{B^b}$ = key signature. The I represents the key.
For example: 1 = B♭, 4 = E♭, 5 = F

. = 1 Beat, in this case a quarter note.

⟍⟋ = Decrescendo (softer)

‖: :‖ = repeat a certain section

> = push the beat

⟋⟍ = Crescendo (louder)

1st
⌐———— = 1st ending

2nd
⌐———— = 2nd ending

— = A dash represents a minor chord.

(D)

Thinking Out Loud

Verse ‖: 1 3̣ 4 5̣ 1 3̣ 4 5̣
        1 3̣ 4 5̣ 1 3̣ 4 5̣

Band In → 1 3̣ 4 5̣ 1 3̣ 4 5̣
Verse   1 3̣ 4 5̣ 1 3̣ 4 5̣

pre-chorus 2-   5 1̣   2-   5
            2-   5 6-   2-   5 ℓℓℓℓℓℓ ⸗⸗

Chorus 1 3̣ 4 5̣ 1 3̣ 4 5̣
         1 3̣ 4 5̣ 1 3̣ 4 5̣
        6· 5 4 3̣   2- 5 1̣ :‖
                  ℓ F F F ⸗

Solo 1 3̣ 4 5̣ 1 3̣ 4 5̣
       1 3̣ 4 5̣ 1 3̣ 4 5̣

Chorus 1 3̣ 4 5̣ 1 3̣ 4 5̣
         1 3̣ 4 5̣ 1 3̣ 4 5̣

Outro 6- 5 4 3̣   2- 5 1̣   6- 5 4 3̣   2- 5 1̣

        6 5 4 3̣   2- 5 ①

(Thinking outloud)

⬚ D = key signature. 1 = D

_____ = 1 Bar with chords evenly split
          unless otherwise notated.

> = represents a push

◊ = represents a whole note

. = (. = 1 beat, in this case a quarter note.)

‖: :‖ = represents repeating a certain section.

‑ = A dash represents a minor in a chord.

Standard Musical Notation Charts

Traditional notation-based charts are seen by musicians all over the world; each country, city, or even district may use a variation on the standard Western music notation vocabulary.

As a session guitarist/sideman, I was fortunate to learn chart writing from New York–based arrangers-composers, including the great William Eaton, Leon Pendarvis, Don Sebesky, and Dick Behrke. Their approach to chart writing was most likely learned/handed down to them by the great arranger-composers from the big band era.

The point in writing a good notation-based chart is the same as writing a good song: communication. Don't make the musicians have to hunt and peck for their specific part or the song form. Lay out your chart cleanly and easy to read. Musicians on bandstands or in studios have no time to waste, and neither do you.

The bane of performing musicians everywhere is the unpreparedness of an artist or songwriter delivering a musical traffic jam of unclear road-map chart information.

Compound this by the fact that good musicians change and enhance arrangements to the benefit of artists and songwriters on the spot all the time (if the artist or songwriter lets them). Also, poorly written charts can be/are vibe killers to the natural giving process of good musicians (another barrier to overcome).

Well-written charts, on the other hand, send signals to the musicians that you know what you're doing, that you're a pro, too. The bottom line: the musicians appreciate your respect of protocol and that will show up in their playing . . .

While reading the notation-based charts, make mental notes of these particular details. They make for a clear, concise road map of the song:

- The song title, artist, and number of page(s) are clearly spelled out on top of the chart.

- The tempo marking and song type are included on the top left side of the page.

- All sections of the song form—verse, prechorus, chorus, bridge—start on the *left* side of the page and are clearly shown as section markings: A, B, C, D, E, etc.

- Each bar of the song is identified: intro bar are lettered: a, b, c, d, e, f, g, etc., and each bar starting with the singer entrance is numbered: 1, 2, 3, 4, 5, 6, 7, 8, etc. (This is done to make it easier to read the music in 8- or 16-bar phrases once the vocal starts.)

- Only the most essential information should be included in the chart. Let the musicians play, adding their magic to the music.

A final suggestion about putting a good chart together: Look to map out the chart prior to writing it, whether in pencil or in whatever music notation software program you're working with.

While listening to a recording of the song you're charting, start to lay out the bar lines on the staff so that the start of each section of the song form—intro, verse, prechorus, chorus, and bridge—are lining up on the left side of the staff they appear on.

Don't commit the entire chart to ink until you've figured out the cleanest, easiest way to lay out the chart for reading.

Here are a few examples of notation-based charts for rhythm sections:

Not Looking For Good Tonight

"THINKING OUT LOUD"

12
Bringing It All Back Home

Bob Dylan changed what people thought pop music was or could be in the early '60s. The musical renaissance he lit a match to gave songwriters permission to write lyrics and make music that had nothing in common with the American Songbook standards of the previous thirty years.

In his Foundation Trilogy book series, science fiction writer Isaac Asimov predicted a future where psycho-historians, via a mathematical formula, could reengineer the future for the benefit of mankind." The future didn't quite work out as planned . . .

Who knows whether the current decade(s) will stand as a musical renaissance. Time will tell. It's up to you, the songwriter reading this book, to aim high and make a difference.

Every generation is entitled to its music: it defines us, as the times do. Still, "the fundamental things apply as time goes by . . ." Emotion remains highest on the list of what to communicate to an audience. The delivery systems change while emotions remain consistent.

Dylan was a song interpreter long before becoming a songwriter. His explanation of how he first got interested in writing his own songs is unique and worth a read in volume 1 of his book *Chronicles*.

When Dylan broke onto the scene as a songwriter, he seemed to know something everyone else didn't. He sounded as if he just came down off the mountain with the Tablets in hand, had just spoken privately with the Fates, had read your mind and dismissed it with a "You've got a lot of nerve to say you are my friend" sneer. In a word, he had authority . . .

Cockiness obviously existed before Dylan, but he took it stratospheric.

What are you taking stratospheric? It doesn't have to be authority, it could be sincerity or any other emotion. Just own it.

Film director Mike Nichols said, "Behind all great art is a secret."

He could have added after "secret" *story, act, betrayal, crime, desire, dream*, or *intention* to that line.

The generator of art, the secret behind its creation or event is the realm of the writer. How or what you choose to reveal, make public or keep private about that secret story, act, betrayal, crime, desire, dream, or intention needs to translate as an invitation for the audience to see their life in your song.

Cole Porter, one of America's preeminent songwriters, literally lived with his secrets due to the public morals that defined his era. His training, talent, ambition, and work ethic took *elegance* stratospheric. His uniqueness as a writer also made him a target for criticism that his songs were "too clever" for general American tastes of the period. Humbug! We don't need a psycho-historian to tell us where Cole Porter ended up in the pantheon of songwriting longevity; he breathes the rarefied air reserved for the genius company of his peers, the greatest songwriters of all time.

Limitations can be a creator's best friend. What looks like a problem is actually a gateway for an ingenious solution. Irving Berlin only composed and played in the key of F-sharp (all the black keys). Did this limitation give him focus? You could make a strong case for it: he wrote over 1,500 songs in F-sharp, too many hits to mention, though "Top Hat," "No Strings (I'm Fancy Free)," "Putting on the Ritz," "Cheek to Cheek," "The Piccolino," and "Let's Face the Music and Dance" make up a few of my favorites.

Did the harsh public treatment of homosexuality, a cultural and/or moral limitation of the times contribute to Porter's urgency to express emotion? That may be a question for a scholar, but it seems reasonable that his private life was on a collision course with social norms of the day, adding another powerful strand of longing to his intense ballads "So in Love," and "Night and Day."

The point is our vulnerabilities can be our greatest strength. (FYI: I'm not suggesting homosexuality is a vulnerability.) The urgency to make sense of the places our vulnerabilities take us, drives good songwriters to the core of what holds meaning for them.

The urgency living in Dylan's "Like a Rolling Stone" and Cole Porter's "So in Love" creates an equal urgency and need in an audience to listen. This cycle of call and response represents the achievement songwriters reading these words should look to attain and carry on.

In the service of the human heart, how high will you aim? What will you give yourselves and the next generation of songwriters permission to do?

For me and the rest of the world, I/we can't wait to listen and find out!

Part Two

Condensed Reference Guide to Songwriting Decision Making

The following condensed reference guide contains the foundational information in *The Elements of Song Craft* in a "Quick Dive" format.

It's designed for writers to easily find useful information, reference materials, or inspiration while writing by themselves or in collaborations.

Song Concept Development
Section I

Developing an instinct for song ideas is a good songwriter's first job. There's a range of tools to help writers review ideas, such as the practice of *keeping a list of song titles.*

As obvious as this is to experienced writers, it's not a common practice for many developing writers.

The benefits of building a song title list are multiple in that:

1. A title itself creates a lyrical destination for a song's chorus—the most memorable part of a song.

2. Just thinking about how to make titles work over the length of a three minute twenty-second song creates the necessity to plan how to best organize and write them.

If we were sitting together in a room, I might suggest we do a round of *song title ideation.* This is where, collectively, writers look at the many ways an idea can be written, then decide which approach works best, both emotionally and creatively for the writer, and for the audience the writer wants to connect with.

Song ideas also spring from:

- Improvising

- Exploring a feeling

- A melody

- A riff or motif

- A few chords or chord progressions

- An inspiration from a beat

- A song you like

- A sound

- A few words read or overheard

- A conversation with a cowriter(s)

- A writing prompt

- An emotion generated by a conversation or confrontation or an inspiration

- Dialogue heard in movies, TV shows, and podcasts are rich fishing grounds for song ideas

- How you feel

- Something you saw

- What's going on in your life at the moment

- A specific prompt: what's the scariest thing that ever happened to you?

Each of our five senses can trigger a memory, idea, emotion. An event can trigger a memory or an expectation.

Some ideas draw on:

- perspective

- time

- the use of objects or values to convey our fears, concerns, and desires

- the point of view (POV) of objects, products, or values to generate unique song concepts

These are all valuable strategies to begin developing ideas with, but at an early stage, it's important to ask: *to what end?*

What are the criteria, the standard that defines a strong song concept? Consider that good songs are often distinguished by:

1. A highly unusual or original way to write an idea

2. A combination of surprise and familiarity

3. A concept that inspires exciting options to write it, such as writing it from multiple points of view or can be easily expressed in vivid personal details, original pictures, and metaphor

4. A deep personal need or urgency to write, driven by strong emotions or a need to explain or come to terms with emotions or events or to celebrate events

5. You found a way to build on or create an original variation from a song you admire by making a slight variation on its idea, title, or concept, such as:

   • As time goes by

   • As tears go by

   • Why can't he be you?

   • Why can't I be her?

Sometimes, we know what we're looking for; sometimes, it's a complete surprise, a gift from the muse. That eureka moment when we're struck by inspiration, a need, a revelation, a premise, or see an opportunity to write a song based on instinct or experience. These moments happen in a flash.

I call them **Creative Planck Time™** moments after German astrophysicist Max Planck, who discovered the rate of speed the universe expanded after the big bang.

Ideas and inspiration also expand in a heart and mind with creative excitement and speed. With experience, we learn to *fully harvest the DNA of our ideas* matching both music and lyrics (prosody) to execute on the creative opportunities alive in our first creative impulses.

Opportunity Briefs and Premises

An effective way to decide the strength of a concept or inspiration is to write a short Opportunity Brief and Premise about the song title or idea you're considering.

Sometimes, our first impulse about an idea is our best; other times, it's worth circling around it and digging a bit deeper. The Opportunity Brief offers that deeper dig to examine all the potential your idea generates beyond a first impulse.

A lot of good decision making gets made at this stage, including:

- What's interesting, original, or exciting about the opportunity to write the idea?

- How easy or hard is the song title to rhyme (how many rhyming opportunities are present in each word of the song title)?

- How easy or hard is the song title to sing (how pleasing or harsh is the sound of the songs title to the ear when sung)?

- Who's the target audience for the song and why will they care about it?

- What song category will the song easily fit into?

- What emotion will the song make an audience feel?

- What song craft tools can be used to fully harvest the idea?

- Doing an Internet search to determine whether the song idea has recently or effectively already been written and how your idea is different, in short an Opportunity Brief, is the intelligence gathering part of songwriting informing us if the song has enough promise or potential to write.

The Premise is the plan to write the song itself once you've decided on the best approach that serves your idea. A Premise should spell out:

- The specific story line or concept you decided the songs about

- How you plan to make the chorus/title line pay off (be interesting or memorable)?

- What song craft tools will be used to develop the story line/song concept across the song form: verse, prechorus, chorus, etc. (the song's beginning, middle, and end)

- What combination of familiar and surprising elements, or stark honesty, might be revealed in the song that enhance, use, or relate back to the song title

- And lastly, what purpose does writing the song serve. Why do you need to write it and how will you invite the audience into the song so they can relate to its message and want to hear it?

The premise is your construction plan to harvest the Brief's intel into a finished song that has legs and staying power.

Creating Opportunity Briefs and Premises for each new song idea might seem a bit much, but it's a worthwhile habit to develop. With a little practice, this turns into mental note taking and part of your natural songwriting process.

Experiment with these approaches; your head and heart will gain new freedom to create and communicate.

◉ Creative GPS: A Formidable Songwriting Construction Tool

Just as GPS works by three vectors intersecting to determine where we are, where our destination is, and how fast we're traveling toward it, so to can this concept be applied to measuring how fast a good song needs to travel toward its destination, an audience.

Our Creative GPS uses four principles (vectors) to guide our decision making. They are:

🧠 Song Intention

The intention is the reason we're writing the song in the first place. What do we want to happen by writing the song?

😲 Core Emotion

What singular emotion is at the song's heart, driving it?

🎵 Song Category

What type of song are we writing? love, breakup, makeup, empowerment, coming of age, party, etc.?

👥 Audience Tracking

What song craft tools are we using to ensure the song is relatable and communicating effectively with an audience across the entire length of the song?

Use Creative GPS while listening to every song you hear and write by identifying the intention, core emotion, and song category driving them. Add the practice of using audience tracking craft tools and your songs will become grounded to higher standards.

Why? Because you're now learning to listen for and building your songs on core communication strategies.

The Elements of Song Craft Creative GPS™

1. **Intention:** What do you want to have happen by writing/singing the song? You're writing the song because you want . . . what?

2. **Core Emotion:** What core emotion is your song built on? What emotion are you feeling that you want your audience to feel?

3. **Song Category:** What song category does the song easily fit into?

Now that you know what kind of song you're writing, let's look at:

4. **Audience Tracking:** Which song craft tools will you use to invite your audience into the song and keep them emotionally hypnotized throughout the **song form**? From **Verse 1**, **Pre-chorus**, **Chorus**, **Verse 2**, **Bridge**, or **Refrain**, how are you balancing creativity and clarity in crafting the songs appeal to your audience?

Underlying Song Craft Distinctions

1. Songs are written as a response to an event.

2. Early in the writing process, make a conscious decision to put yourself on the "listener's" side of your song.

3. Standards matter! You're in the communication business. How well are you communicating your intention?

A "Deep Dive" into Advanced Song Craft Perspective Tools

Song Intention

- Songs are written as a response to an event

- Song Concept Development

- Ideation strategies

- Premise and Brief:

  Premise: The research into ways to write the idea/emotion.

  Brief: The plan/roadmap of how you'll harvest your best approach to write the song across the song form.

Core Emotion

Emotions powering songs include: Joy, Loss, Hope, Reassurance, Grief, Swagger, Regret, Forgiveness, Longing, Gratitude, Rejection, Acceptance

- Connected to your need to write it with

- An audiences need to hear it

♫ Song Category

Is your developing song a:

- Devotional love song

- Empowerment song

- Break up song

- New love song

- Coming of age song

- Song of reassurance

- Song of forgiving or asking for forgiveness

- Political song

- Authority song

- Attitude or swagger song

- Dance song

- Party song

- Etc.

👥 Audience Tracking

What song craft tools are you using (across the song form) to keep your audience emotionally committed to keep listening throughout the song?

- Are you balancing creativity and clarity?

- Are you using The Lyrical Grammar™ editorial tools of:

  - Summing-Up™

  - Shrink-Wrapping™

  - Perspective Tools - Invitations

  - Harvesting Song DNA™

  - Calculating Distance to Target™

  - Making distinctions about the kind of song you're writing: inspirational or entertainment; intention based or free association?

- Are you using musical and lyrical momentum strategies and contrast tools in shaping your song throughout the song form?

- Are you using the melodic construction tools of Step, Rhythmic, and Intervallic Driven™ melody creation across the song form?

- Are you using images, writing with pictures that are sticky to create a state of Emotional Hypnotism™?

Sixteen Song Title Ideation Strategies

Along with Opportunity Briefs, Premises, and Creative GPS, these ideation strategies give writers more choices in deciding the types of songs that can be written and how to best develop the ideas that drive them.

Thinking about song titles this way leads to greater creativity and a framework to speed development of the song itself through each part of the song form (first verse, prechorus, chorus, second verse, chorus, bridge, and outro).

Lyric and melodic development tied to song form is a critically important concept to grasp and exercise. Much as an on-time train arrives at each stop of its route on schedule, so too can a song lyric and melody be written to arrive on time at key places in a song to keep its momentum up and the audience involved throughout.

If you already have a title in mind to write, skip the Genesis Line Strategy and start with the Debate Team Strategy. While debating, scan the entire list for additional inspiration and opportunity to write your song.

1. **The Genesis Line Strategy**™—Is where you come up with a title or write the whole song based on the inspiration generated from one line or song title. Examples: "Cake by the Ocean," "24 Carat Magic," "Our Love Is Here to Stay," "The Race is On," "Hella Good." This approach typically leads to the genesis line being used at the start and end of a chorus in the AABABCA song form, ("You've lost that loving feeling") or as the first and last line of a song, ("Yesterday") or as a "tagline" song. Where the title is "tagged" onto the last line of a chorus, verse, stanza, or refrain ("Cake by the Ocean"). Once you've settled on a song title, run it through the other strategies/see which provides the best avenue for self-expression and an audience's connection to the song.

2. **The Debate Team Strategy**™—Is where you weigh or debate a number of ways to write the idea, the song premise (based on the genesis line/song title) and choose which approach best suits the writer and the song. Sometimes this includes making the song a "story song" and all the benefits that storytelling offers to songwriters (including all the advantages that come from structuring a beginning, middle, and ending).

Other times, we might debate the various or contrasting points of view available to write the song from. For example, the following titles could be written two ways:

- Example One: "You're Gonna Need a Bigger Heart" can be written from a *universal space*: to ask people to give more of themselves to make the world a better place as the state of the world demands each of us care or do more to make the world a better place, or

- Example Two: "I'm Gonna Need a Bigger Heart" can be written from a more *personal space*: the need for the singer or writer to make room in his or her own heart to forgive a friend or lover's transgression. Another example:

- Example Three: Ariana Grande's "Problem" featuring Iggy Azalea. The song was a huge success the way it was written, but as an example, it could be written a few ways. The way "Problem" was written was using the title to say, 'I should leave you, I'd have one less problem without you if I did but I want you, so even though the relationship has gone bad, we're still hanging out.' This way it's a "disillusionment with love" song. That's valid for the song and audience it's aimed at.

- Example Four: "Problem" could also be written as an empowerment song by debating/writing the idea (genesis line) from the point of view of the woman actually ending the relationship and now, "I got one less problem without you," spells out she ended the relationship and is free of the problem and because of that decision, new, more promising opportunity has opened up!

3. **The Problem-Solution Setup**—Is a technique for using a verse to illustrate a "Problem" then a chorus to illustrate the "Solution" to that problem. "You've Got a Friend" performed by Carol King is a good example. This approach also works in reverse, whereby a chorus illustrates a problem (for example, how bad a breakup feels), with a verse contrasting/illustrating how good the relationship once was.

4. **The Environmental Strategy**—Is where all five senses are used to create visual images, storytelling/metaphors, similes, and analogies to write a song. For example, Joni Mitchell's "Chelsea Morning," "Both Sides Now," and Rodgers & Hammerstein's "My Favorite Things."

5. **"The Vignette Strategy**—Is where each verse tells a different story or vignette connected by the chorus. Again, Joni Mitchell's "Both Sides Now" or Dawes's "A Little Bit of Everything, Ty Herndon's "A Man Holding on to a Woman Letting Go," Leonard Cohen's "Everybody Knows" are good examples of vignette strategies in action.

6. **Single-Word Titles**—Songs like "Help," "Belief," "Try," "Torn," etc. Owning a word, a name, or place as in a single-word title is a lofty goal for songwriters to aim for.

7. **Songs with "Action(s)" in Their Title**—"Living on a Prayer," "Working My Way Back to You," "If It's the Last Thing I Do," "Every Breath You Take."

8. **Songs with One Word Changed in Their Title**—"As Time Goes By"–"As <u>Tears</u> Go By"; "Rhythm of the Night"–"Rhythm of the <u>Sun</u>."

9. **Setups: Making Comparisons or Conclusions**—"Our Love Is Here to Stay": "In time the Rockies may crumble, Gibraltar may tumble, they're only made of clay, but our love is here to stay." "All of Me": "You took the part that once was my heart, so why not take all of me." Also, "Summertime Blues."

10. **The Tag Line Song**™—Is where the title is "tagged on" to the end of a verse or refrain. Examples include: Prince's "When Doves Cry," Billy Joel's "She's Always a Woman to Me," Bryan Adams's "Everything I Do," Chick Rains and Wade Hayes "Old Enough to Know Better," Bob Dylan's "Gates of Eden."

11. **The Sandwich**—Is where the title is used at the start of a stanza, verse, or chorus and is repeated at the end of a stanza, verse, or chorus. Songs such as "Yesterday," "I Fall to Pieces," "Where Is Love?" Alan Jackson's "I Don't Even Know Your Name."

12. **The Authority Song**™—Are songs where you sound like you know something no one else does. Songs such as Bob Dylan's "Like a Rolling Stone," or "The Times They Are A-Changin', Jimi Hendrix's "The Wind Cries Mary."

13. **The Reveal**—Is where the song has a lyrical emotional surprise, or twist. This is typically used in the tag line song format where the title is "tagged on" to the last line of a verse, stanza, or chorus. Songs with strong reveals include: Logic's "800-273-8255," in which the title is not even sung in the song, or Larry Boone, Paul Nelson, and Richie McDonald's "Everything's Changed," Performed by Lonestar, Hank Cochran's "Why Can't He Be You," Ray Davis's "Lola," Jamie O'Hara's "The Cold Hard Truth," Shel Silverstein's "A Boy Named Sue," Don Schlitz and Paul Overstreet's "When You Say Nothing At All." (performed by Keith Whitley and Alison Krauss).

14. **Novelty Titles**—Is taking places, events, famous characters from real life or fairy tales, stories, history, or mythology and finding ways to turn them into song titles, also double-entendres: "Every Cinderella Has Her Midnight," "Alice, This Ain't Wonderland," "Boys Lie, It's Something in Their Jeans," "I'm Victoria's Secret."

15. **Singing "Stream of Conscious"** words, syllables, and sounds to a melody line or track. This free association approach has yielded some very famous songs and is used by many successful songwriters.

16. **Mirror Writing Strategies**—Writing original lyrics to the rhythm and rhyme scheme of a well-known song, then creating an original melody and chord pattern to match the mirror written lyrics. Writing an original melody and lyric over a preexisting set of chord changes.

The Elements of Song Craft Mastery Strategy Chart

Communication achieves emotional hypnotism.

Songs are written as a response to an event. What do you want to say about that event?

Is your intention to inspire or entertain?

SONG CATEGORIES/TYPES OF SONGS BUILD SONGS ON CORE EMOTIONS

Inspiration Songs:

- Love: New Love / Devotional / Make Up / Break Up
- Songs of Longing: Loss / Grief / Hope / Forgiveness
- Coming of Age
- Songs of Reassurance
- Empowerment Songs
- Joy: Songs of Remembrance / Romance
- Songs Based on Coming to Terms with an Event
- Songs of Regret / Revenge / Rejection / Gratitude

- Chants
- Children Songs
- Alienation / Freedom
- Anthems / Authority Songs
- Socially Conscious Songs

Event Or Holiday Songs:

- Christmas / Valentines
- Celebration Songs

Entertainment Songs:

- Party Songs
- Dance Songs
- Summer Songs
- Authority Songs
- Political Songs
- Attitude Songs: Swagger / Defiance / Confusion

Harvesting Song DNA / Song Title Ideation and Concept Development Strategies

- Genesis Line Strategy™
- Debate Team Strategy™
- Environmental Strategy™
- Single Word Song Titles
- Vignette Strategy™
- Authority Songs
- The Reveal
- Songs with Action Words in Their Titles
- Title Sandwich
- Changing One Word in a Famous Title

- Writing Your Greatest Fear
- Titles that Make Comparisons
- Intention Based or Free Association Song Strategies™
- Call—Answer Writing Strategies
- Song Form / Tag Line Strategy™
- Singing Stream of Conscious Words and Melodies
- Topline to Track
- Writing Your Greatest Joy
- Collaboration Strategies

ADVANCED SONG CRAFT STRATEGIES

Lyrical:

- Grammar Tools™

- Editorial Tools

- Song Craft Perspective Tools

- Brief and Premise Strategies

- Creation Space vs Re-Write Space™

- Problem - Solution Tied To Song™

- Object / POV Strategies™

- From POV of Time, Values, Products

- Reverse Lyric Study™

- Musical and Lyrical Momentum

- Musical and Lyrical Contrast

- Balancing Creativity with Clarity

- Song Asset Lists

- Creative GPS™

Melodic and Musical:

- Melodic Reverse Engineering

- Melodic Profile™

- Step, Rhythmic, and Intervalic Approaches

- 3, 4, and 5 Note Motif Strategies

- Chromatic and Diminish Motion Studies

- Bass Line Driven Songs

- Intro Motif Driven

- Major to Minor Key Verse / Chorus

- Song Form Usage and Strategies

The Usage Rule Guide
Section II

Usage Rules for Lyric Creation

1. Good songs are written as *a response to an event*. Know your intention, what you want to have happen by writing about that event. Know it early in the creative process.

2. Tied to *intention* is an opportunity to harvest everything related to your original desire, need, or interest to write a song; all related emotions, details, stories, visuals/pictures, and meaning inherent in its idea and title should be used in its creation (harvest your song's DNA). Write the song's DNA as opposed to leapfrogging to ideas or images that are unrelated to it.

3. Develop and maintain *a list of song titles* that represent your ideas. Use the titles on that list as the lyrical destination for your song's chorus or tag line (the last line in your verse or refrain).

4. Songs are typically designed for two main purposes, *to either inspire us or entertain us*. Know which one your song's designed to do. (Some can do both simultaneously.)

5. Good ideas can be written in many ways; that's what makes them good. Review your song idea and title thoroughly. Think through various ways you could write the idea, especially from different or contrasting points of views or a surprising point of view. Settle on the best approach to the idea based on honesty—what's happening or has happened in your life—or on the entertainment value of the idea. (Use the Opportunity Brief/Premise approach.)

6. When you don't know what to write next in a lyric, ask yourself this question: *I'm writing/ singing this song because I want . . . what?*

7. Writer's block or not, finishing songs is typically due to *writers' mistaking or not knowing what their song is really about.* If you experience writer's block, meditate on the event at the root or reason you're writing the song, then on what you need to say about that event and what emotion you want to express and want the audience to feel. For example, you may think you're writing a breakup song about rejection, but the song might really be about a history or pattern of rejection. Opening that door could lead to finding a richer or truer theme to base or on which to finish the song.

8. Good songs have one *core emotion* at their core driving them. The sooner you know what that core emotion is, the sooner you'll know which lyric, ideas, and concepts support the song and which don't. These core emotions are typically:

   - Hope

   - Joy

   - Loss

   - Longing

   - Regret

   - Grief

   - Gratitude

   - Longing

   - Reassurance

   Knowing the core emotion also defines the emotional response an audience feels when listening to a song. (Learn the Song Arts Academy's Critiquing System, identifying key emotions driving songs, in chapter 1.)

9. Smart songwriters know which song category they're working in early in the writing process. Knowing the type of song you're writing allows writers to organize their lyric writing around the core emotion related to that category.

For example, devotional love songs are typically driven by the emotion of commitment, whereas coming-of-age songs can be driven by the emotion of a longing for a lost sense of freedom.

Song categories include but are not limited to:

- Empowerment
- New love
- Breakup
- Makeup
- Disillusionment with love
- Reassurance
- Feel-good moments
- Party
- Regret
- Gratitude
- Cockiness
- Revenge
- Coming-of-age
- Devotional love
- Longing or soul
- Authority

10. A good song works because *the audience knows who to root for*; they instantly identify with the singer, and *see their life in the song* or like the story. You need to know what's at stake for you singing your song so that the audience will instantly know *what's at stake* for them to keep listening to it.

    Honesty and vulnerability are essential to great songwriting.

    Make a conscious choice to write your songs keeping the listener's perspective in your thoughts while writing. Do that and they will be riveted and keep listening.

11. Your goal is to be a communication expert. That's the main business you're in as a songwriter. Remain vigilant and honest to see when you are or are not communicating your song's intention clearly or can communicate it better. The proof of your communication expertise lies in your audience clearly understanding your intent.

12. Look to achieve **Emotional Hypnotism** of your audience through the premeditated use of ideas, concepts, and advanced song craft techniques.

    An audience becomes hypnotized when the writer removes thinking from the audience's experience and allows pure feeling and reaction to drive the listener's involvement in a song.

    In chapter 2 and 3 are editorial and clarity tools that help sustain the hypnosis process.

13. How you use time; the present, past, and future plays a crucial role in good songwriting.

    Write in the moment as if the revelation of what you're writing about just hit you.

    This creates a tremendous need for you to write the song, and as a result, an *equal need* for an audience to listen and keep listening to the song.

14. Aim to become a **Songwriting Athlete**, meaning build perception (the songwriting muscle) though the everyday exercise of being present in the moment by writing dozens to hundreds of songs.

    By applying craft to experience, songwriters develop a unique sensitivity or athleticism to report back to an audience what's most meaningful about the world around us all.

15. Consider there are two prime style approaches with which to write a song. One is *intention-based* songwriting, the other is *free association-based* songwriting.

16. Intention-based songs are written from the starting point of knowing what and *why they're being written.*

    Examples of intention-based songwriting:

    - Cole Porter's "So in Love"

    - The Beatles' "In My Life"

    - Sara Bareilles's "Brave"

17. Free Association Songs are based on metaphor, random line writing, or highly *suggestive images that produce a unique mood,* or a Rorschach test–type response in a listener.

    Examples of free association-based songwriting:

    - Procol Harum's "Whiter Shade of Pale"

    - The Beatles' "Lucy in the Sky with Diamonds" and "The Walrus"

    - Jillette Johnson's "Butterfly Catcher"

18. When to best use first-, second-, and third-person POV in a song? First person POV is effective in writing songs of personal discovery.

    For example:

    - REM's "Losing My Religion"

    - Hank Williams's "I'm So Lonely I Could Cry"

    - Julia Michaels' "Issues"

Second-person POV is a smart choice especially when deciding when to use *you* as opposed to *he* or *she.*

For example, Billy Preston's song "You Are So Beautiful to Me" would be less effective if it was "She Is So Beautiful to Me," because now we have to *think* about who "she" is.

It turns out the use of "you" is a *trigger* to quickly grab a listener's attention, as people interpret "you" as themselves—and we are always our favorite subject—as opposed to "he" or "she" (third person), which makes an audience have to think about who "he" or "she" is.

Making your audience feel is almost always a better choice than having them think when it comes to songwriting. Third person POV—he, she, they—seems to be best used in story songs or songs where the narrator *is relaying a story to the listener:* the Beatles' "She's Leaving Home," or Sara Evans's "Suds in the Bucket" are good examples of third person usage.

19. *Write your life*: what you're experiencing right now, what you've experienced in the past, and what you may imagine in your future.

Write the scariest, happiest, most rewarding, funniest, most vulnerable moments you've lived through. You can do this as an exercise or as a song you don't finish or play for anyone. Writing goals like these stretch and strengthen your writing muscles.

20. *Pictures are sticky*; statements are often less so.

Aim to be a visual storyteller. Why? Because songs are typically first experienced as audio; live, or over loudspeakers or earphones.

An audio speaker is not a TV or video monitor. It is not a *visual* medium. So, the lyrics need to be visual so that your audience can easily "see" your message and their life in your songs. That makes for real connection, impact, and staying power.

21. Use objects in your lyric writing. Either as tools to exploit your intention (see chapter 8) or as in writing a song from the point of view of an object.

This gives songs added emotional power, originality, and dimension by introducing unusual or novel elements of surprise. This can also be applied to writing songs from the POV of a value; for example, "The Cold Hard Truth."

22. *Song form* is valuable as a *lyrical momentum* tool. There are critical junctures/pivot points lyrically in a song's form and structure where songs either take off or fall flat.

These junctures in the AABABCB song form are typically:

- The first two lines of the start of a verse

- The prechorus

- The start of the chorus, and at end of it if it includes the song title

- The start of the second verse

- The start of the bridge

23. *Lyrical momentum* needs to develop constantly throughout a song. There are many writing perspectives and tools to help a writer keep a song's momentum moving. They include:

- The use of musical and lyrical contrast (see chapter 4)

- The use of problem-solution setup (page 28 under Title Ideation Strategies)

- The use of perspective shifts between verse and chorus

- The use of **Lyrical Grammar**: a two-line couplet strategy where one line is driven by metaphor and the second line is a clarifying statement (supporting the use of the metaphor)

  For example, "That hill is now an on-ramp to an interstate" (an image)

  Time leaves its stamp on all things in its wake (a statement)

- The use of summarizing why you've said what you've said at critical junctures

24. *Make your song lyrics smaller*, not larger.

   Meaning, make your lyrical picture(s) specific (smaller), not too general or so wide (larger) that the lyric loses potency.

   For example, such words as *love, pain, something,* and *it's* are often too general. What love? What pain? What something are you referring to?

   These are examples of what I call Empty Calorie Words. Strive to use images, metaphors, similes, allusion, and allegory or write statements that vividly show what *love, pain, this, thing, something,* or the *it's* you refer to.

25. When writing pictures, use your five senses to describe the environment you're in. Describe in the moment emotions. Also use the sixth sense:

   - Premonition

   - Kinesiology

   - Magic

   To heighten urgency in a song, write pure "action commands" in a chorus. A good example of this is Ed Sheeran's "Thinking Out Loud."

26. Don't take for granted that the audience understands *what your song is about.* What's vividly clear to you in your head, what you've written, is not automatically vivid to your audience.

   Use the device of summarizing, Summing Up what you've written, tied to song form (see chapter 3).

27. Urgency: Your urgent and deep need to express emotion in the moment is a prime factor in winning and keeping audiences deeply involved in your song.

28. Your verse and chorus should have *opposite contrasts*: If the verse states a *problem*, the chorus should state the *solution* to the problem, or vice versa. Carole King's "You've Got a Friend" is a good example of this.

29. Use the passage of time in writing your songs. Write in the present (in the moment), the recent past, or the distant past to convey urgency, momentum, and longing.

30. Leave out all the stuff no one wants or needs to hear in your songs.

31. The secret to a well-written song is that the second verse is better written than the first verse.

32. Memorable lyrics use objects to represent a character's emotions, mental state, and intention (see chapter 8).

33. Good songs have a clear destination, a finish line.

    Spell out that finish line, the reason you're singing your song.

    Many writers merely point at a list of general or somewhat related details in their lyrics, thinking the audience will instantly understand their significance or meaning. They don't.

    What is clear in your head is not guaranteed to be clear to an audience.

34. A bridge or refrain is typically where writers circle back and literally let the audience know why the song was written.

    It's the last opportunity writers have as a communications expert to connect the reason they wrote the song—what you wanted to gain, point out, or have happen—and tie it up in a bow to deliver to your audience.

Usage Rules for Melodic Development and Song Construction

Melody, Song Form, Chords, Bass Lines, Music Creation

1. There are three core types of melody writers

   - Step

   - Rhythmic

   - Intervallic

   Good melody writing employ all three approaches.

   Most writers are typically strong in one of these categories. Ask yourself which group you naturally fall into and work on improving the other core types.

   ### Three-Core Melody Definitions:

   - **Step melodies** are melodies that move in a stepwise motion up and down the scale in close proximity to one another. Step melodies typically stay within a modest vocal range. Good examples are:

      - "Heart and Soul"

      - James Taylor's "Fire and Rain"

      - "Where Is Love?" from the musical *Oliver!*

   - **Rhythmic-driven melodies** are exactly as they sound; distinguished by rapid or repetitive rhythmic movement. Examples are:

      - Taylor Swift's "Bad Blood"

      - Pharrell Williams's "Happy"

      - Irving Berlin's "Puttin' on the Ritz"

- **Intervallic melodies** are melodies distinguished by either large-scale-degree jumps between notes, sometimes an octave or slightly less up and down the register, or by smaller (ear-catching) chromatic movements. The following songs are examples of melodies with large interval jumps:

  - "Somewhere over the Rainbow"

  - "I Know I'll Never Fall in Love Again"

  - "How Do I Live"

- The following songs are examples of smaller interval or chromatic intervallic movement:

  - "White Christmas"

  - "If This Isn't Love" (from the musical *Finian's Rainbow*)

  - "James Bond Theme"

2. Practice writing melodies based on *three-, four-, or five-note repeating motifs* in two-bar phrases. Many great writers do, so why not you!

   - Melodies built on three-note rhythmic motifs:

     - "She Loves You"

     - "Let It Snow"

     - "All of Me"

     - "Baby Love"

     - "Yesterday"

     - "All Night Long"

     - "Missing You"

     - "I Like It, I Love It"

- Melodies built on four-note rhythmic motifs:

  - "Can't Buy Me Love"

  - "Mr. Sandman"

  - "Autumn Leaves"

  - "Satisfaction"

  - "I'm Your Venus"

  - "There's Your Trouble"

- Melodies built on five-note rhythmic motifs:

  - "Every Breath You Take"

  - "Bad Blood"

  - "It Had to Be You"

  - "Strangers in the Night"

  - "I'll Be Seeing You"

  - "That'll Be the Day"

  - "It's Now or Never"

  - "Please Mister Postman"

  - "I Love Rock 'n' Roll"

  - "A Broken Wing"

  - "Breathe"

3. Understanding song form helps writers become persuasive communicators. Why? Because since the dawn of time, our ancestors have been making and listening to music using common song forms, such as verses, chorus, and bridges, so unconsciously that song form is hardwired into our historical memory and DNA, the same as language and grammar.

    Smart songwriters take advantage of song form because they know primarily they are in the communication business and song form is a prime musical communication tool.

    People subconsciously understand the elements of repetition and surprise contained in song form.

    Song form is typically expressed in the letters:

    - A B C: A = verse

    - B = chorus

    - C = bridge

    Song forms can also include such terms as:

    - Introductions (intros)

    - Verse

    - Prechorus or channel

    - Chorus

    - Refrain

    - Middle eight

    - Coda

    - Outro

    - Hook

Song form and its use in popular music changes radically over time.

A few typical song form examples are expressed as:

- AA "This Little Light of Mine" (traditional)

- AABA The Beatles' "Yesterday" and Billy Joel's "Just the Way You Are"

- AABABCB James Ingram's "Just Once"

- AABCABC Sia's "Chandelier"

What's important to know for developing writers is the opportunity that using these forms presents specifically how they allow the song to quickly connect with an audience.

For example, songs written in AABA form typically puts the song title at the end of the sung phrase or verse. I call these **Tag Line Songs**, as the song title is "tagged on," or added as the last line sung in the phrase.

The tag line form creates the wonderful opportunity to turn the whole verse; everything sung leading up to the tag line, *into a chorus.*

This is a popular song form used for years as it makes for very memorable melodies to thrive. Oftentimes, adding the title to the opening line of the song and then "tagging it" on to the last line, makes a song more memorable, as is the case with the Beatles/Paul McCartney's "Yesterday."

If your focus is writing for today's pop music market, you'll need to deliver four to six undeniable rhythmically driven vocal hooks. The structure of a song like "Thinking Out Loud" is an excellent example:

4. Song form matters. Emotions that drive lyrics typically stay *stable* over time; song form changes from generation to generation. What was called a verse in the 1950s bears no resemblance to what is referred to as a verse today.

5. Syncopation changes over time. Each new generation redefines rhythm. Compare a '20s New Orleans jazz band's syncopation to '60s funk, '80s pop, or current musical and melodic rhythm.

6. Just as New York City real estate has become insanely expensive, so has the real estate of lyrics and musical hooks in pop songs.

   Attention spans are short, bridges and prechoruses too plodding. They've been replaced by catchier, rhythm-driven melodic hooks, memorable musical hooks that stand on their own, hooks almost or as strong as the song's main chorus.

   If you're writing current pop, you better deliver four to six great hooks per song.

7. Many contemporary songs use repetitive, four-chord progressions to build on. Sometimes, these progressions move in such a way as to never point to an exact key center.

   These are called ambiguous *chord center progressions*.

   They create a lot of musical uncertainty.

   The progression in Katy Perry's "Wide Awake" is an example. Its progression of G11, B-flat2, F, and C would indicate that F is the song key, but the song never resolves/lands on F.

   Chord progressions cycling over in this fashion complement lyrics about alienation or disillusionment. (Note: when playing this progression, keep the note C on top of each chord.)

8. Sing-song melodies are a reality in pop music. The familiarity of response and hookiness are factors in their use as unifying anthems. Also, pop music is much like any other corporate-driven business, and corporations are obsessed with growth.

   Growth in the music industry tends to come from attracting younger audiences, perhaps a contributing factor in why so many nursery rhyme–type "woah-oh" sing-along parts are heard in contemporary songs.

9. Memorable melodies thrive on *contrast and repetition*. Writing long-held notes contrasted by short, punchy rhythm-driven notes in your hooks or contrasting verse and choruses is a smart strategy to use. The same is true for notes sung loud or soft for contrast.

10. There are interesting and surprising chords that can be substituted for many standard chord progressions. A study of the music theory of substitution chords for tonic, dominant, and subdominant chords are:

Chord Families	Chord Degree	Theoretical Name	Example (C Major)
Tonic	I	Tonic	C
	IIIm	Mediant	Em
	VIm	Submediant	Am
Sub-dominant	IV	Subdominant	F
	IIm	Super Tonic	Dm
Dominant	V	Dominant	G
	VII°	Leading Tone	B°

11. Bass lines (*root motion*) play a huge role in defining melody and rhythm. Train yourself to listen and identify the bass parts in songs; become aware of their harmonic and rhythmic movement.

For example; harmonically, John Lennon was and Paul McCartney is a genius in writing simple descending bass lines to shade and enrich the beauty and simplicity of their melodies ("Lucy in the Sky with Diamonds" and "Michelle"). So was Cole Porter' in "It's Alright with Me," and countless other writers and arrangers.

On the rhythmic side, think:

- Bruno Mars's "Uptown Funk"

- The System's "You're in My System"

- SDG's "Gimme Some Lovin'"

- The Knack's "My Sharona"

- Stevie Wonder's "Sir Duke"

- Gamble & Huff and Anthony Jackson's "For the Love of Money"

- Berry Gordy and Janie Bradford's "Money (That's What I Want)"

The list of bass-line driven songs and hooks goes on and on . . .

12. *Bass lines are hooks.* Take advantage of knowing that and not overlooking the opportunity to create them when needed.

13. Utilize a technique to generate original melodies by reverse-engineering well-known "public domain" melodies.

This is accomplished by taking a well-known melody and reversing it so the second part of the melodic phrase is sung first and the first part of the melodic phrase is sung last.

Add an original chord progression to support the reverse melody and experiment.

This technique is used as a jumping-off point for inspiration, not a license for any unauthorized use of copyrighted material.

Song Critique Checklist

1. Creative GPS Tools and Song DNA Harvesting

   - Apply all four components of Creative GPS when reviewing how successful a song's *Intention*, *Core Emotion*, and *Song Category* has been communicated, written, and harvested.

   - Note which *Audience Tracking* "Advanced Song Craft Tools" were used in writing the song.

   - Note what other Advanced Song Craft Tools or Ideation Strategies might also have been used to write it.

   - Note where the writer "harvested the song's DNA or Song Title" throughout the song or missed opportunities to do so.

2. Communication: Balancing Creativity with Clarity

   - On a scale from 1 to 10 (10 being the high score), how successful is the song's balance of Creativity to Clarity (*Surprise* to *Familiarity*)?

   - Where in the song form (or at which lines) did you have to "think" what the song was about?

   - Where in the song form (or at which lines) did you "feel" or "know" what the song was about?

   - How well has the writer balanced the use of *relatable* images, pictures, or metaphors to outright statements?

3. Use of Lyrical Grammar and Editorial Tools

   - When reading a song lyric, where do you notice in the lyric the writer used Lyrical Editorial Tools to write the song concisely?

   - What other Lyrical Grammar and Editorial Tools could have been used in writing the song?

4. Song Form: Melodic and Lyrical Development

- How well has the writer tied the song's melodic and lyrical development to the song form?

- Does the song's melody keep rising higher throughout the song form climaxing at the chorus?

- Is there unique, memorable, "hooky" melodic contrast in the song? How is the combination of step, rhythmic, and intervalic melodic motion used in the song tied to the song form?

Usage Rules for Rewriting Songs

The Creation vs. Rewrite Space

A quote attributed to Sir Paul McCartney is: "Your song's not finished till you hear it on the radio."

All or most experience songwriters are dedicated *rewriters*. The time to circle back from initial inspiration to determine the quality of a developing song demands scrutiny.

1. Rewriting is where you take thinking out of your song and replace it with feeling, momentum, and contrast. Some of the most relevant elements to add may have been overlooked in the rush to start writing the song.

    There are two distinct writing spaces in songwriting, the **Creation Space** and the **Rewrite Space**.

2. In The Creation Space, you're focused on getting a toehold on an idea/concept, a melody, chords, and words so they flow in the general direction of your idea, passion, inspiration, craft, and lucky creative accidents.

    Your frame and focus is on getting something going, not on scraping the excess glaze off the finish.

3. When rewriting, listen back to your song with a critical ear; it's your job to notice every songwriting decision.

    Learn to clearly see and hear the contributing factors to the drag on your song's momentum—those extra melody notes, for example. You may have needed those notes to be able to write the melody, but now, in the rewrite phase, they need to be removed. Why? Once they are gone, the melody will be easier to remember, the phrase will breathe better, and the song will be easier to sing.

4. This holds true for *extra* words. All those extra words (including "I"; everyone knows it's you singing) can also now be removed. Extra words can distract from the Emotional Hypnotism needed to make your song memorable.

5. The same applies to tempo and musical accompaniment. The tempo at which you wrote the song will most likely prove too slow for the final version, even though it was great during the "writing mode" as your *hunt-and-peck* tempo to learn how the song should go.

6. Same holds true for accompaniment. That first guitar or piano part you came up with served you perfectly as a songwriter, but now the demands of finishing a song must fit within an arrangement, or with other players, current production, and programming styles.

7. Consider the value of rewriting. Nearly every song played on the radio or streamed is highly vetted. *Learn to love rewriting.*

    Become your own best gatekeeper. Give the real music industry gatekeepers more reasons to like your song, because you understood the realities of good songwriting; you rewrote your song as many times as it took to make it good.

Additional Song Concept Critiquing Tools and the Elements Vocabulary List
Section III

Let's marry title ideation with an Opportunity Brief and Premise strategy to critique and analyze "Cake by the Ocean," by the band DNCE, using a Genesis Line Strategy.

Good genesis lines are dependent on the song title having a payoff, a logical reason why they are sung. Let's look at the lyrical mechanics of "Cake by the Ocean":

The Genesis Line Strategy Applied to Critique of "Cake by the Ocean"

Song Title: "Cake by the Ocean" ▶

The chorus genesis line: "Cake by the Ocean"

Opportunity Brief: The opportunity to write "Cake by the Ocean" is to create a *fun, party, dance song*. Great! People love and need to party.

The title is a *picture* and has both familiar and surprising elements. That's smart, we're going to remember it: the title stands out. The title is also easy to *sing and rhyme*.

Allegedly, the title came from one or two of the Swedish writers who were working on it misunderstanding the term *sex on the beach*. (FYI: Sex on the Beach is the name of a cocktail.) Well, that worked out well for everyone involved.

Let's look at the **Premise**, the logic the writers came up with to make the song title lyrically make sense.

Premise: This is a party, come-on, looking-to-hook-up song. A boy wants to get close to a girl, chides her for being too serious when they could be having fun getting to know each other, with his ultimate aim being to have "cake by the ocean." Translation: getting romantically or physically closer, perhaps leading to sex on the beach.

📍 Critiquing "Cake by the Ocean" using the Creative GPS (Intention, Core Emotion, Song Category, Audience Tracking)

🧠 Song Intention

To convince a girl to relax, not to be too serious, have fun, enjoy the party and perhaps more . . .

😩 Core Emotion

Hope ("I keep on *hopin'* we'll eat cake by the ocean")

🎵 Song Category

Party/dance song

👥 Audience Tracking

What song craft strategies are used in "Cake"?

- *Problem-Solution Setup*

  Verse shows the problem: you walking 'round like it's a funeral

  Chorus shows the solution: go fucking crazy eat cake by the ocean

- *Summing Up*

  By using the lyric: But you're moving so carefully, let's start living dangerously

  The writers sum up the essence of the first verse before starting the chorus

- *Adding Surprising Elements*

  "Waste time with a masterpiece" is such an iconic line, it's catchy and surprising.

- *Smart use of Harvesting Song DNA*

  The writers stick with the concept in outro adding types of cake to be eaten.

Lyrical Momentum: An Introduction

Just like an airplane, a certain momentum must be achieved at critical times to make your song take off. Let's take a look at song form/song structure, line by line, section by section, and see where momentum is most critical.

The Verse

Opening Line

The first line must be compelling: either intriguing, exciting, brutally honest, poetic or sexy/entertaining. (Simply, it's got to contain a reason that compels the listener to stick around to listen to the second line.)

The First Payoff

The listener is becoming emotionally involved in what's developing and will keep listening.

The Prechorus

In the prechorus, momentum is gained by:

1. Developing the idea from the verse further

2. Introducing an idea that leans the listener toward the idea/song title to be introduced in the chorus

3. Introducing a new idea

The Last Line of the Prechorus

The last line of the prechorus is your best opportunity to set up your chorus. How do we do that? With momentum:

1. Make a bold statement.

2. Write a line that carries the thought of the line before it to a "heightened" commitment or conclusion.

3. Surprise the listener with contrast.

The Chorus

The Second Payoff

The downbeat of the chorus is where your song takes off (pays) or crashes. The reasons songs fly:

1. Brilliant, original idea: "The song remembers when"

2. A catchy phrase with great rhythm: "Who let the dogs out"

3. Passion and poetry; a huge need to express real and/or raw emotion: "No place that far"

4. You said something everyone wants to say or have said it to them in an honest or unique way: "I can't make you love me."

5. The release is so satisfying and infectious YOU'RE HOOKED!

The Second Verse

The challenge is to find new relevance, a new creative vein to tap, or just really good lines in the same vein as the first verse. What really needs to be said next? Why is it important? Does it say the same thing (as in the first verse) in a different way, or can it say something different in a way not introduced before? Bottom line: keep the listener involved with the development of the song.

Notes on the use or nonuse of a second prechorus: Many well-written songs often drop a second prechorus (after a second verse) for the simple reason of getting to the chorus faster.

The Bridge

Either:

1. Sums up or ties up the point of the song

2. Is a contrast to the main statement of the song, à la the Beatles' "WE CAN WORK IT OUT . . . life is very short and there's no time," etc.

Also keep in mind:

The Reasons Songs Crash

- Bad idea

    1. It's not original.

    2. It's not relevant to anyone.

    3. It's been done a million times and better than your attempt

- Poor execution

    1. Bad crafting

    2. Poor communication skills: you know what you mean, but no one else does.

Analysis of "Chandelier" Using the Elements of Song Craft Momentum Grid

The following "Momentum Grid" example of the song "Chandelier" shows, line by line, the development over the song form. Listen to the song while reading the lyrics on the grid.

"Chandelier" ▸

Written by Sia and Jesse Shatkin

SONG FORM: ABCDABCD

Line Count/ABCD Song Form Indicator	HOOK COUNT
VERSE 1 (A)	H1

   1. **Party girls don't get hurt**

   2. **Can't feel anything, when will I learn**

   3. I push it down, push it down

   4. I'm the one "for a good time call"

   5. Phone's blowin' up, they're ringin' my doorbell

   6. **I feel the love, I feel the love**

PRECHORUS (B)	H2

   7. **1, 2, 3, 1, 2, 3 drink**

   8. 1, 2, 3, 1, 2, 3 drink

   9. 1, 2, 3, 1, 2, 3 drink

  10. **Throw em back, till I lose count**

CHORUS (C)   H3

11. <u>**I'm gonna swing from the chandelier, from the chandelier**</u>

12. <u>**I'm gonna live like tomorrow doesn't exist, like it doesn't exist**</u>

13. <u>**I'm gonna fly like a bird through the night, feel my tears as they dry**</u>

14. <u>**I'm gonna swing from the chandelier, from the chandelier**</u>

REFRAIN (D)   H4

15. <u>**And I'm holding on for dear life,**</u>

16. won't look down won't open my eyes

17. Keep my glass full until morning light,

18. <u>**cause I'm just holding on for tonight**</u>

19. Help me, I'm holding on for dear life,

20. won't look down won't open my eyes

21. Keep my glass full until morning light,

22. <u>**Cause I'm just holding on for tonight, On for tonight**</u>

VERSE 2: (A)

23. <u>**Sun is up, I'm a mess**</u>

24. Gotta get out now, gotta run from this

25. <u>**Here comes the shame, here comes the shame**</u>

PRECHORUS (B)

CHORUS (C)

REFRAIN (D)

How to Read the Momentum Grid

Weighing the Importance of Each Line in a Song

Each line of a song is important; that said, due to where a line falls in the song form, some lines are more important than others in creating *momentum* throughout a song.

1. A song's opening line(s) draw a listener in so its value is higher than some other lines.

2. Lines that have more value than others are shown in larger text and are <u>underlined.</u>

3. The most important momentum or payoff lines are shone in even larger text and are <u>underlined</u>

4. The line count indicates how many "original lines" exist in a song. Important to note that *repetition* plays a huge role in creating song momentum.

5. Hook Count: Within the context of meeting standards for popular radio–driven songs, hook counts of 4 to 6 are common. *Hooks* in this context means memorable sung lines or sections of songs.

6. Song Form: For the purpose of clarity, I make a distinction of each section of a song being represented: V = A / Pre = B / Chorus = C / Refrain or Bridge = D

7. Note the role that *repetition* plays in well-crafted songs. "Chandelier," for example has only 25 original lines in it. The pre-chorus, chorus, and refrain/bridge all repeat.

8. Note where lyrical contrast is used to create momentum in "Chandelier". Again, contrast is also tied to song form.

9. Note what's "left out": The second verse is half as long as the first. This is typical in radio pop songs as getting back to the chorus quicker is paramount.

From reading the Momentum Grid, it's easy to see that the main areas where momentum is achieved are in the opening and closing lines of each part of the song form, the verse, prechorus, chorus, and bridge/refrain. Use the Editorial/Lyrical Grammar Tools in this book to help in achieving the required momentum for your song lyrics.

A Final Note on Momentum

There's no place to coast in a song since the form is so short. You've got to get a lot of work done quickly and honestly while staying true to the emotion/idea that drives the composition. There's no room for equivocating in a smart, well-written song.

The Elements of Song Craft Vocabulary List

Terms Used in Song Arts Academy Training

The Song Arts Academy (SAA) offers songwriting workshops, masterclasses, and private training. The SAA has enjoyed long-term support for developing songwriters from ASCAP, BMI, and SESAC.

These vocabulary terms make distinctions and frame creative ways of thinking about songwriting. Experiment by adopting them when talking about songs and by applying them in writing the prompts in *The Elements*.

1. Emotional Hypnotism™: A state produced by a well-written song. A state of emotional reaction when thinking is replaced by a listener's emotional response.

2. Intention Based Songwriting™: Songs written from the starting point of knowing what and why you're writing them.

3. Free Association Songs™: Songs primarily based on metaphor, random line writing, or suggestive images that produce a Rorschach test–type response in a listener.

4. Song DNA™: A term describing closely related essences, elements, or opportunities present in a song idea, title, or emotional proposition.

5. Harvesting Song DNA™: Fully exploiting or writing every part of a song's potential as defined by its title, idea, or emotion, using song craft to connect with an audience based on:

   - Knowing the event you're writing about

   - Knowing why you're writing the song

   - Knowing what you want to have happen by writing the song

   - Knowing why an audience will care about the song

   - The use of original metaphors, similes, analogies, analogs, images, and statements—picture-driven storytelling—inherent in or related to the song's concept

6. The SAA Critiquing Method™: A strategy to critique as well as build songs based on a singular core emotion, intention, and Song Mechanics™

7. Creative GPS™: A term describing four components (vectors) used in Intention Based Songwriting to gauge the strength and direction of a song in development. The components are:

- Knowing your Intention; why you are writing the song and what you want to happen by writing the song

- Focusing on the Core Emotion driving the song; for example, hope, loss, regret, joy, reassurance, etc.

- Understanding the Song Category a song falls into; for example, devotional love, coming of age, party, empowerment

- Audience Tracking™: Tracking the use of various song craft tools that insure an audience stays listening to a song throughout the song form.

8. Creative Planck Time™: A term that describes a writer's growing excitement in the initial moments of inspiration when exploring the potential of musical or lyrical ideas for a song. (Based on German theoretical physicist Max Planck's discovery of the rate of universal expansion after the big bang.)

9. Creative Clarity™: A term used to describe the balance between a writer's poetry skills and their song craft communication skills.

10. Lyrical Grammar™: An umbrella term for the editorial tools Summing Up™ and Lyrical Logic™.

11. Summing Up™: Spelling out exactly what you meant in a lyric before adding a new idea or concept to that lyric. Summing Up is usually tied to song form usage; the meaning of four lines of a verse is "summed up" or spelled out in two lines of a prechorus, for example.

12. Lyrical Logic™: Revealing what a metaphor means by following it with a clarifying statement. Usually used in a couplet where the first line is a metaphor and the second line is a statement explaining emphatically why the metaphor was used.

13. The Shape of Your Heart™: A term used to describe the unique emotions, stories, and ideas that resonate with each individual writer. A term to help writers determine which ideas, themes, and emotions are most powerful to write.

14. Emotional Transactions™: A term used to describe a writer's ability to be present to witness and report back/write about the range of experiences going on around them in daily life.

15. Songwriting Athleticism™: The practice of exercising advanced song craft every day in your songwriting to build perception and being present in the moment.

16. Growing Your Ears™: Developing a sensitivity to recognizing the smart decision making renowned songwriters use in putting their songs together then applying them in your own.

17. Opportunity Brief™: A list of mental notes or research regarding the viability, originality, or practical realities of developing a song idea in its infant stages, including:

   - Assessing the value of the song idea/concept

   - Creating a list of words that rhyme with the title.

   - Determining best approach to write the song from

   - Your intention: assessing your reason and need to write the song and what do you want to "happen" by writing and singing the song (emotional movement)

   - How original is your approach?

   - Googling the song title for history of idea

   - Who is the song's audience? Why will this audience want to hear the song over and over again?

18. Song Premise™: A short written synopsis of the story line or the plan to how to best write a song with the information revealed in a song brief

19. OPMC (opportunity, perspective, momentum, and contrast): Advanced song craft skills used in determining the quality of your song ideas and best practices to write it while under construction.

Acknowledgments

Much thanks to Deidre Sullivan for suggesting there was a book in my material and for the introduction to my agent. To Janet Rosen, Sheree Bykofsky, Phil Wild, John Cerullo and Clare Cerullo for their expertise and insights in guiding the *Elements* into readers' hands. Thank you, Carolyn Fagan, for research, managing the manuscript, and initial line edits; you make me look good! Sincere thanks to Iris Bass for copyediting and to William Linster, Dav Abrams, Jon Buscema, Paul Scholten, Alexander Kaletski, Joe Hudson, Mark Burschfield, and Agostino Bellocco, for their help in preparing and reviewing parts of the manuscript.

A big shout-out to my professional friends and colleagues in New York, Nashville, and Los Angeles Samantha Cox, Charlie Feldman, Robbin Ahrold, Gene Seidman (interstitial design elements), Brandon Haas, and the entire creative team at BMI, Jamie Dominguez, SESAC John Titta, ASCAP Linda Lorence Critelli, Trevor Gale, Qian "CC" Liu, Tabitha Fair, Randi Michaels, Rand Bishop, Steve Leslie, Phil Barnhart, Kathy Anderson, David Malloy, Steven Sharf, Caroline Bienstock, David Preston, Del Bryant, Paul Lewis, Dr. Martin Mueller, Dr. Ron Sadoff, Stephen Webber, Alex Hyman, Matt Carlson, William Gillett, Maria Caso, Kristin Gardner, Sebastien Raoux, Amy Tarr, Chris Palmaro, Bashiri Johnson, Rich Mercurio, Oz Noy, Hanan Rubinstein, Robert Ellis Orrall, Pablo Munguia, Mike O'Rear, Donna Hilley, Don Pfrimmer, Arjun Roy, Tim Pattision, my parents Nancy and Murray, sister Kate, brothers Peter, Dan, and Gene. Finally to the hundreds of collaborators I've written and write with and the thousands of students who've worked with me; you grace my creative life every day . . .

About the Author

Billy Seidman is a respected songwriter, musician, producer, and educator. His songwriting career includes staff positions at RCA Music Publishing, Warner-Chappell Music Publishing, SONY/ATV Tree Music Publishing, and Carlin America Music Publishing, in New York and Nashville. He's an adjunct professor of songwriting at NYU, Steinhardt Department of Music and Performing Arts Professions, the New School for Jazz and Contemporary Music, and a consultant for Berklee NYC/ The Power Station.

His songs have been recorded and performed by Oscar-, Grammy-, Emmy-, Golden Globe–, and Tony-winning artists, including Irene Cara, Vicki Sue Robinson, Evelyn "Champagne" King, Kevin Kline, and more. Hit makers Bebe Rexha, Alisha "M'Jestie" Brooks, and Rachel Platten have studied with him. He's the founder of Song Arts Academy, a New York–based songwriting school supported by ASCAP, BMI, and SESAC.

His song catalog is available for licensing at: broadjam.com/songs/billyseidman.

The author can be contacted at:
billy@billyseidman.com
billy@songartsacademy.com
https://www.facebook.com/bside11
https://www.instagram.com/bside11/

Music Credits

Alcohol
Words and Music by Brad Paisley
Copyright © 2005 Spirit Catalog Holdings, S.à.r.l. and
New Sea Gayle Music
This arrangement Copyright © 2019 Spirit Catalog
Holdings, S.à.r.l. and New Sea Gayle Music
All Rights for Spirit Catalog Holdings, S.à.r.l. Controlled
and Administered by Spirit Two Nashville
All Rights for New Sea Gayle Music Administered by
ClearBox Rights
International Copyright Secured All Rights Reserved
Reprinted by Permission of Hal Leonard LLC

Alfie
Theme from the Paramount Picture ALFIE
Words by Hal David
Music by Burt Bacharach
Copyright © 1966 Sony/ATV Music Publishing LLC
Copyright Renewed
This arrangement Copyright © 2019 Sony/ATV Music
Publishing LLC
All Rights Administered by Sony/ATV Music Publishing
LLC, 424 Church Street, Suite 1200, Nashville, TN 37219
International Copyright Secured All Rights Reserved
Reprinted by Permission of Hal Leonard LLC

All Of Me
Words and Music by Seymour Simons and Gerald Marks
Copyright © 1931 Sony/ATV Music Publishing LLC,
Round Hill Songs, Marlong Music Corp. and Bourne Co.
(ASCAP)
Copyright Renewed
This arrangement Copyright © 2019 Sony/ATV Music
Publishing LLC, Round Hill Songs, Marlong Music Corp.
and Bourne Co. (ASCAP)
All Rights on behalf of Sony/ATV Music Publishing LLC
Administered by Sony/ATV Music Publishing LLC, 424
Church Street, Suite 1200, Nashville, TN 37219
International Copyright Secured All Rights Reserved
Reprinted by Permission of Hal Leonard LLC

Alone Again (Naturally)
Words and Music by Gilbert O'Sullivan
Copyright © 1972 Grand Upright Music Ltd.
Copyright Renewed

This arrangement Copyright © 2019 Grand Upright Music
Ltd.
All Rights Administered by Sony/ATV Music Publishing
LLC, 424 Church Street, Suite 1200, Nashville, TN 37219
International Copyright Secured All Rights Reserved
Reprinted by Permission of Hal Leonard LLC

Anyone Who Had A Heart
Lyric by Hal David
Music by Burt Bacharach
Copyright © 1963 BMG Rights Management (UK) Ltd.
and New Hidden Valley Music
Copyright Renewed
This arrangement Copyright © 2019 BMG Rights
Management (UK) Ltd. and New Hidden Valley Music
All Rights for BMG Rights Management (UK) Ltd.
Administered by BMG Rights Management (US) LLC
All Rights Reserved Used by Permission
Reprinted by Permission of Hal Leonard LLC

Better Now
Words and Music by Austin Post, Carl Rosen, Adam Feeney,
Louis Bell, William Walsh and Kaan Gunesberk
Copyright © 2018 SONGS OF UNIVERSAL, INC.,
POSTY PUBLISHING, ELECTRIC FEEL MUSIC, EMI
MUSIC PUBLISHING LTD., MYNY MUSIC, SAM FAM
BEATS, EMI APRIL MUSIC INC., NYANKINGMUSIC,
WMMW PUBLISHING and KAAN GUNESBERK
PUBLISHING DESIGNEE
This arrangement Copyright © 2019 SONGS OF
UNIVERSAL, INC., POSTY PUBLISHING, ELECTRIC
FEEL MUSIC, EMI MUSIC PUBLISHING LTD.,
MYNY MUSIC, SAM FAM BEATS, EMI APRIL MUSIC
INC., NYANKINGMUSIC, WMMW PUBLISHING and
KAAN GUNESBERK PUBLISHING DESIGNEE
All Rights for POSTY PUBLISHING and ELECTRIC
FEEL MUSIC Administered by SONGS OF
UNIVERSAL, INC.
All Rights for EMI MUSIC PUBLISHING LTD., MYNY
MUSIC, SAM FAM BEATS, EMI APRIL MUSIC INC.,
NYANKINGMUSIC and WMMW PUBLISHING
Administered by SONY/ATV MUSIC PUBLISHING
LLC, 424 Church Street, Suite 1200, Nashville, TN 37219
All Rights Reserved Used by Permission
Reprinted by Permission of Hal Leonard LLC